repentance to Life
another look at the new birth

Christine L. Steiner

repentance
to Life
another look at the new birth

repentance to Life: another look at the new birth

by Christine L. Steiner

© 2007 Word Aflame Press
Hazelwood MO 63042-2299
Cover design and layout by Ben Meydam

Unless otherwise identified, all Scripture quotations in this book are from the New King James Version®, Copyright © 1982 by Thomas Nelson, Inc. Used by permission. All rights reserved.

Scripture quotations marked NIV are taken from the HOLY BIBLE, NEW INTERNATIONAL VERSION®. NIV®. Copyright © 1973, 1978, 1984 by International Bible Society. Used by permission of Zondervan Publishing House. All rights reserved.

Scripture quotations marked AMB taken from THE AMPLIFIED BIBLE, Copyright © 1965, Zondervan Publishing House. Used by permission of Zondervan Publishing House. All rights reserved.

Song "Lonely River" on page nine used by permission.
Copyright ©1996 Careers-BMG Music Publishing/Magic Beans Inc. (Admin. BMG Music Publishing) / O'Ryan Music
©1997 Sony/ATV Tunes LLC, Deer Valley Music, Familiy Reunion Music and Magic Beans Music. All rights on behalf of Sony/ATV Tunes LLC and Deer Valley Music administered by Sony/ATV Music Publishing, 8 Music Square West, Nashville, TN 37203. All rights reserved. Used by permisssion.

All rights reserved. No portion of this publication may be reproduced, stored in an electronic system, or transmitted in any form or by any means, electronic, mechanical, photocopy, recording, or otherwise, without the prior permission of Word Aflame Press. Brief quotations may be used in literary reviews.

Printed in United States of America

WORD AFLAME PRESS
8855 Dunn Road, Hazelwood, MO 63042
www.pentecostalpublishing.com

Library of Congress Cataloging-in-Publication Data

Steiner, Christine L.
    Repentance to life : how we through the Gospel come from death to life / Christine L. Steiner..
       p. cm.
   ISBN 978-1-56722-711-6
   1. Repentance—Christianity.   I. Title.
BT800.S74 2007
234'.5—dc22   2007015326

To my girls,
Adrienne, Ashley, Amber, and Alicia

"All your children shall be taught by the LORD,
And great shall be the peace of your children"
(Isaiah 54:13).

My utmost thanks to my Father and Savior, Jesus Christ.

"Write in a book for yourself
all the words that I have spoken to you"
(Jeremiah 30:2).

acknowledgments

I want to thank Sister Mullins for allowing the Lord to use her in the confirmation on this project and for all the prayers and support she and Brother Mullins gave to me through this journey in my life.

To all my family and friends who prayed and supported me through this journey and project. Thanks, Sisters Vicky Harger and Patricia Bollmann, for editing this book. You were good to me.

Last but not least, to my mother for saying yes to the call of God to serve Him. It has allowed my brothers, sisters, and me to have a hope in knowing Jesus Christ. We have been spared death to have abundant life in Jesus Christ. Thanks!

Lonely River

Lonely river
You meander like a road
Stretching out into the great unknown
With solitary movement
You're compelled and you're enthralled
As though you're answering a distant call

Lonely river
Is there a place you're running to
Or is it something that you're running from
Is it hope that keeps you going
Is it faith that makes you strong
Lonely river, lonely river, running on

Lonely river
In the stillness of the night
Your restless nature keeps you raging on
Changing courses
Shallow waters, tangent streams
Lonely river, do you wonder what it means

Lonely river
I think I am a lot like you
Winding on in hopes to find the sea
And flooded by uncertainties
The current can be strong
But drifting towards our destinies
The arm of God is long
And I believe that through this journey
Till we're finally home
Lonely river, we will never run alone

To all who go through this life in the uncertainties that it brings, you and I can have hope that we will never run alone.

contents

Foreword		13
Preface		15
1. Celebrating Christ's Birth		25
2. Celebrating Christ's Death		33
3. Celebrating Christ's Resurrection		41
4. The Godhead		51
5. The Gospel According to the Scriptures		77
6. The Promise of Spiritual Birth		83
7. The Promised Holy Spirit		91
8. The Promise Has Come		97
9. How the Disciples Obeyed		103
10. And They Continued in the Apostles' Doctrine		109
11. The Samaritans Received the Living Water		117
12. Paul's Conversion		125
13. That They May Receive Forgiveness of Sins		133
14. You Are Abraham's Seed, and Heirs		141
15. Repentance to Life		149
16. The Gentiles Should Hear the Word		157
17. Did You Receive the Holy Spirit When You Believed?		163
18. Conclusion		175
Notes		183

foreword

Only by divine revelation can we understand the truth of who Jesus Christ is. *Repentance to Life* unfolds the significance of repentance and the revelation of the Godhead. Only God can reveal Himself, and He has obviously done so to Christine Steiner. This subject is vital, and we can benefit by allowing this book to open our understanding so we can enter a vital relationship with Christ by walking in true repentance.

When we first moved to Nebraska to pastor the Apostolic Christian Church, Christine Steiner was a very shy, reserved individual. Her spiritual growth has caused all areas of her life to blossom, and the Lord has empowered her with holy boldness. Her confidence in God has multiplied and her faith has been transformed into that of a mighty oak.

It has been my privilege to observe Christine's spiritual progress. She is a faithful wife, a good mother to her four daughters, a mighty prayer warrior, and my friend. Thank you, Christine. May all who read this book come to true repentance.

Alice Mullins

preface

Repentance to Life was birthed through difficult circumstances in my life, circumstances that were not of my doing but were designed for my arriving at a deeper understanding of truth.

In August of 2000, as we came back home from a family vacation, for some reason I was troubled about needing to lose the weight I had gained during my latest pregnancy. One day as I gnawed at the problem, a distinct and emphatic inner voice seemed to say, "You are going to lose thirty pounds." *Where did that come from?* I wondered. Little did I know that my subsequent weight loss would not be inspired or supervised by Jenny Craig or Dr. Atkins but by God.

After this initial encounter, my emotional and spiritual landscape began to change. I felt unsettled and uncomfortable. I felt a kinship with David when he said, "Why are you downcast, O my soul? Why so disturbed within me?" (Psalm 42:5, 11; 43:5, NIV). Looking back, I now can see that God was getting me ready to venture with Him into uncharted territory, but at the time I had no idea where the road would take me or what would happen. It felt like something was wrong, and I prayed constantly, whether in my mind or on my knees.

During one of my prayers, the Lord told me He wanted me to enter into a season of fasting. I answered by promising I would fast on a regular basis for six months if He would help me. I did not know exactly why I would be fasting, because I had not quite figured out what was wrong. However, I did ask for wisdom.

Preface

I had fasted before for different things, but this new experience was without parallel. When I started in January 2001, I wondered how often I was supposed to fast, but when I stopped trying to do God's job, I knew exactly the days to fast and did not worry about it any more.

As time went on, I fasted and prayed earnestly, but the unsettled feeling was still there. Then the road turned into a quagmire. I did not understand that God was trying to get me to see that the source of my uneasiness was my need to better understand my Holy Spirit baptism and the oneness of God. My journey stopped as my feet bogged down in miry confusion. I had been in the church for twenty-six years, but everything I thought I knew about my faith went from me. It seemed like God had abandoned me on the lonely road in a dark and howling wilderness.

I wanted to scream and run away, but my feet were stuck. Alone and afraid. I wished I were dead. It was my darkest, most frightening experience, and I wanted out. But I knew that if I gave up, I would be the loser. There was only one way to go: straight ahead.

I did not want anyone to know about my dark muddle; in any case, I did not really know how to explain it. I searched for God as I continued to fast and pray. During one church service I felt the Lord nudging me to talk to Alice Mullins, the pastor's wife. I told Him I did not want to talk to her because I did not want to reveal my uneasiness and confusion, but I made a concession. I did not want to draw attention to myself by approaching her in the sanctuary, so I told the Lord, "I am going to the restroom, and when I come out if she is not in the sanctuary, then I will talk to her." Our church had two women's restrooms, and when I left the sanctuary, the pastor's wife was still sitting in a pew. When I came back to the sanctuary, she was not there. Just as I approached the other restroom door in search of her, she came out. I told her I needed prayer. She told me that a few days before God had impressed her to pray for me. I was relieved that God had not forsaken me as I had imagined.

I started a journal. When a verse of Scripture impressed me, or God did something for me, I wrote about it. However, this did not provide much relief from my dilemma. The only rest I had was during the few hours I managed to sleep at night. Whenever I awoke, I would be nose to nose with the problem sitting like a boulder on my chest.

I had bought a book about fasting so I could understand its purpose and how to do it properly. I found fasting to be refreshing and exciting because it helped me to stay focused on the Lord. I regret that I did not write in my journal every time I fasted, so I have no record of how many days I actually did fast. I hope it was forty days in all, as many days as Jesus fasted when He was in the wilderness.

In March I wanted to start studying the Godhead, but I did not know where to begin. Everything I thought I knew about Jesus was gone, and I had to start all over again. I was scared, but I prayed for the Lord's help. Still, the uncertainty was frightening. I opened up a little to Pastor Larry Mullins, telling him what was happening to me. But I told him I did not want him to tell me about the Godhead—I wanted Jesus to show me. The few people I spoke to about my questioning of my faith told me that the process was good for me. I struggled to understand how this could be true, because I was scared and felt so alone.

The New Testament seemed to confuse me, so I started my study in Isaiah 1. As I read, I kept track of all the names of God, such as Holy One, Redeemer, Savior, Lord, and King. When I had read to chapter 46, I added the baptism of the Holy Spirit to my study of the Godhead. I found myself going back and forth between the two subjects and became more at ease reading in the New Testament.

Preface

I spent every spare moment reading and praying. Praying was not always easy for me. Many times I felt alone and cried out to God not to forsake me. Many times I asked Jesus to touch me, especially my hands. One day I was in church praying with my hands raised toward heaven as far as I could reach. As I talked to the Lord, I suddenly felt Him touch my hands. Though gentle, His touch startled me, and I pulled away.

As the end of the six months of fasting approached, it seemed like I was still stuck in the quagmire. Summer camp meeting was coming up, and I decided to attend Wednesday through Friday. I told God that if I was making the effort to attend I wanted Him to talk to me. I did not care how He did it, but I needed to hear from Him.

Wednesday night my girls and I attended the camp meeting. I expected to hear from God, but nothing happened. I was discouraged. On Thursday I talked to a visiting missionary and opened up to him a little. My dark time was still hard to talk about, but I wanted so much to talk to someone who could give me the answers. I often felt like God was not teaching me fast enough. As the evening service began, I struggled to enter into the spirit of worship. But when the evening speaker got up to preach, the struggle left. I listened with a hungry heart as he preached about the love of God. When he finished I went up to pray with my hands raised towards heaven, praying in the Spirit. I did not know what I was saying, but I was communicating with Jesus. The missionary I had visited with earlier came up to pray with me. When he was done I felt someone else praying for me but did not know who it was. When I finished praying, I went back to my seat to get my Bible. A lady came up to me and said, "The Lord wants to use you. Don't fear change. Leave the things you've been praying about at the altar and don't pick them back up. God will give you the answers you need in His time." I recognized her voice as the second person who had prayed with me. She did not know my situation or me. I had wanted God to speak to me, and He used her to do it.

As June came to an end so did my time of fasting. On the morning of July 1 this phrase came to mind: "Everything's going to be fine." I took that as a promise from the Lord, and little by little I have seen it come to pass. In October, I went to the doctor. When I asked him what I had weighed at the time of my last appointment the year before, it was thirty pounds more than what I weigh now. This reminded me that the Lord knows things we do not know. I would never have tried fasting as a diet strategy, and during the six months of fasting I was so focused on God and my confusion that I had forgotten about His prediction that I would lose thirty pounds.

After the six-month season of fasting, the Lord began opening my understanding a little at a time to the Scriptures. He gave me a clear understanding of the two subjects I was questioning. For example, one day I had been studying Nicodemus's encounter with Jesus in John 3. I had my Bible, concordance, and notebook paper spread on the floor. After studying and praying, I got up to wash the dishes. As I stood at the kitchen sink with my hands in the warm, soapy water, God told me to go back and read the chapter again.

I dried my hands and started reading slowly at John 3:1. The first seven verses glided past without capturing my attention, but when I started reading the eighth verse the Lord opened my understanding and breathed new life and hope into me. "The wind blows where it wishes, and you hear the sound of it, but cannot tell where it comes from and where it goes. So is everyone who is born of the Spirit" (John 3:8). Everyone who is born of the Spirit would hear the sound it was making! No one could know where the Spirit came from or where it went, but he would hear it. My mind went directly to Acts 2:1-4. I had read these verses many times, but it took the Lord to open my understanding that the "sound" I made, as the Spirit entered my being, was speaking with tongues.

God continued to open my understanding to the Scriptures. While I studied John 14:16, He nudged me to look up the meaning of the word *comforter*. I thumbed through the concordance until I found that it means "intercessor, consoler, and advocate." My heart raced with excitement as I turned to Isaiah 53:12: "He bore the sin of many, and made intercession for the transgressors." *Consolation* means "exhortation, encouragement, and comfort." My heart quickened when I realized that Jesus was doing the same thing for me that Paul promised God would do for believers through His Word: "For whatever things were written before were written for our learning, that we through the patience and comfort of the Scriptures might have hope" (Romans 15:4). *Advocate* also means "exhortation, encouragement, and comfort." In John 14:16, Jesus referred to the Holy Spirit as the "Helper" who would enable believers to understand God and His Word. I was so excited that it was finally happening to me!

It did not stop there. In John 14:26 Jesus said, "But the Helper, the Holy Spirit, whom the Father will send in My name, He will teach you all things, and bring to your remembrance all things that I said to you." There was only one Holy Spirit, and Jesus was claiming to be the Holy Spirit! They were one and the same. I told the Lord: "Jesus, I know you're the Son, and now I know without a doubt that you're the Holy Spirit, but how are you the Father?" The Lord took me to Matthew 1:18, 20: "She [Mary] was found with child of the Holy Spirit. . . . 'For that which is conceived in her is of the Holy Spirit.' "

When a man impregnates a woman, that man is the baby's father. If the Holy Spirit conceived a child in Mary, then the Holy Spirit was the Father. If the Holy Spirit was the Father of that

Son, and Jesus was the Holy Spirit, then Jesus was the Father. This truth led me to Matthew 28 where Jesus declared that all power had been given to Him, and He commanded His disciples to "go . . . and teach all nations, baptizing them in the name of the Father, and of the Son, and of the Holy Ghost" (Matthew 28:19, KJV). I now was sure that this name was Jesus. "Then Peter said unto them, 'Repent, and let every one of you be baptized in the name of Jesus Christ for the remission of sins; and you shall receive the gift of the Holy Spirit'" (Acts 2:38). This led me to Colossians 2:9-10: "For in Him [Jesus] dwells all the fullness of the Godhead bodily; and you are complete in Him."

As the Lord revealed Himself to me, I called the pastor and shared my joy with him. More than once, I suggested to him that I should write a book, but I would laugh it off. However, as I continued to write in my journal, the idea of a book began to gel in my mind.

One night during this time, I had a dream. I was in a church service listening to a sermon. One phrase the preacher said stayed with me after I awoke: "Repentance to life." I knew that if I ever wrote a book the title would be *Repentance to Life*.

I want to relate another scriptural setting God brought to my attention. Two of my children had the flu, and they were both sleeping on the couch. While it was quiet, I picked up my Bible and opened to Acts 15. That evening after the children were in bed, I was dozing on the couch when I heard the words "bare them witness" so distinctly that I woke up. The next morning I went back to Acts 15 to find out what the Lord wanted me to see. Verse 8 drew my attention: "And God, which knoweth the hearts, bare them witness, giving them the Holy Ghost, even as he did unto us" (Acts 15:8, KJV). I read the verse very slowly so the meaning would sink in. Peter was talking to his Jewish brothers about the Gentiles' conversion to which Peter was a witness. God, who knows the heart,

Preface

gave the Gentiles a witness, an evidence that they had received the Holy Spirit. My question was, *What was the witness—the evidence—and what did He show them?* He showed them that He accepted them, and the witness—the evidence—was that they spoke with tongues. The King James English phrase "bare record" has the same meaning. John the Baptist "bare record, saying, I saw the Spirit descending from heaven like a dove. . . . he that sent me to baptize with water, the same said unto me, Upon whom thou shalt see the Spirit descending, and remaining on him, the same is he which baptizeth with the Holy Ghost" (John 1:32-33, KJV). John saw the Spirit descending upon Jesus. This was a witness to John so he could identify Jesus to the world as the One who would baptize with the Holy Spirit. John saw the evidence.

That night, as my children were climbing into their pajamas, I heard a train whistle. I said to God, "I know that's a train because I recognize its sound. Is that the way it is with the Holy Spirit?" I tucked the kids in bed and then crawled between my own sheets. While I lay in bed the words "upon whom you see the Spirit descending" came to my heart. The next morning I found the phrase in John 1:33, the same verse I had found the day before. When a person is baptized with the Holy Spirit, he or she will bare record—or witness—of it. At Cornelius's house in Caesarea, Peter told the Jewish brethren that the Gentiles had received the Holy Spirit "just as we have" (Acts 10:47). How did Peter know that the Gentiles had received the same Holy Spirit the Jews had received? Because they heard them speak with tongues (Acts 10:46). Back in Jerusalem, Peter recounted the event and recollected Jesus' words: "'John indeed baptized with water, but you shall be baptized with the Holy Spirit.' If therefore God gave them the same gift as He gave us when we believed on the Lord Jesus Christ, who was I that I could withstand God?" (Acts 11:16-17). We can see and hear when one has been baptized with the Holy Spirit (Acts 2:33).

Each time the Lord quickened His Word to me, new life and hope bubbled up inside. I wrote a Bible study about my exciting discoveries: true salvation and the true identity of Jesus Christ. I showed the Bible study to my pastor and laughingly reminded him of my suggestion that I write a book. The next day I felt the need to pray. I went into my room, and as I started praising the Lord, the book idea came to my mind. I told the Lord that I did not know how to write a book. I did not think I could do it, but if He would help me I would try. While praying, I felt impressed to talk to the pastor's wife about it but was reluctant to bother her. However, when I finished praying, I called her. We talked for probably an hour, but I did not mention that God wanted me to write a book until we were getting ready to hang up. She replied, "I knew you were going to say that." I laughed and told her I needed her help. We talked about it for a while. After we hung up I assumed that her husband had mentioned my writing enterprise to her. A few days later my curiosity overcame my reluctance, and I called her back. When I asked her how she knew I was going to talk to her about the book, she told me it was not her husband who had told her, but God. That was enough witness for me! I would do what God said I could do.

As I write this preface, it has been two years since the Lord used Alice Mullins to help me understand that God wanted me to write this book. Yes, He gave me a greater understanding of truth than I had before, and I am still seeking and learning. It was a hard-fought battle. The Lord helped me to understand that I had to "win" my own faith in two main areas: He wanted me to understand my salvation and who He is. My prayer and my goal for this book are to help people see the spiritual truths that I found.

As I was writing this book, my daughter Alicia asked where the pictures were. Yes, I am creating a picture not with illustrations but with words. My daughter Amber asked why I used the

Bible so much and if I was going to write my own opinions. When it comes to salvation my opinions do not matter. The only thing that matters is what the Bible says. I wanted to write a book that even my children could understand. I did not want to make these biblical truths complicated, for Jesus said, "Unless you are converted and become as little children, you will by no means enter the kingdom of heaven" (Matthew 18:3). I found through personal experience that God gives light and understanding to simple-hearted believers (Psalm 119:130).

chapter one

Celebrating Christ's Birth

Celebrating Christ's Birth

I love to think about the birth of Jesus Christ. A story that never gets old. Every year as the Christmas season nears and I prepare to tell the story to my family, I am reminded that celebrating Christ is the principle activity of the season. This year was the thirtieth celebration of my rebirth in Christ and the fortieth celebration of my natural birth. But His birth should be cause for the greatest celebration of all. This thought is uppermost in my mind as I write this chapter.

The Son of God and the Son of Man

When I think about the life of Christ—His birth, death, burial, resurrection, and return—I see nothing but celebration for those He has redeemed. It excites my soul, and for that I am truly grateful. The genealogies in Matthew 1 and Luke 3 show that Jesus came from the tribe of Judah, and *Judah* means "celebrated" or "praise." Jesus Christ's birth evoked great joy and celebration. The long-awaited Messiah was conceived by a virgin who had found favor with God. What an honor for Mary to be the means whereby God was manifested in flesh! However, the honor came from God, not man. The very fact that Joseph was troubled about Mary's pregnancy and was thinking about "[putting] her away secretly" tells us that there were ripples of consternation in the community. When Mary said "yes" to God, it meant she had to face her family and the community with the news of her pregnancy. Sometimes the ones who are closest to us are the ones who refuse to believe anything great can come from us.

repentance to Life

The angel Gabriel came to Mary and said, "Rejoice, highly favored one, the Lord is with you; blessed are you among women!" (Luke 1:28). This announcement was cause for rejoicing; the angel assured Mary she need not be afraid. He explained that the Holy Spirit would cause her to conceive and bring forth a son. Mary believed the angel and trusted God as she submitted to His plan. She told Gabriel, "Let it be to me according to your word" (Luke 1:38).

Six months earlier, an elderly priest named Zacharias had finally been chosen to offer incense in the Temple. This was a service a priest could do only once in his career, and it was a great moment for Zacharias. He and his aging wife Elizabeth had experienced few joys, as Elizabeth had never been able to have children. As Zacharias breathed prayers and burned incense at the altar, Gabriel suddenly appeared and told him that Elizabeth would give him a son and that they should name the baby John. John would be great in God's sight and his ministry would spark widespread revival in the land to prepare the way of the Lord. Dumbfounded, Zacharias asked for a sign, and Gabriel told the doubtful priest he would not be able to speak until the child's birth.

Elizabeth was related to Mary. Mary knew about Elizabeth's pregnancy and the story behind it. She knew that Elizabeth would believe her own miraculous story and they could rejoice together, so she went to visit her relative. When the older woman heard Mary's greeting, the baby in Elizabeth's womb leaped for joy. Contrasting Mary's simple faith to Zacharias's doubt, Elizabeth said, "Blessed is she that believed: for there shall be a performance of those things which were told her of the Lord" (Luke 1:45).[1] Seven hundred years before Mary was born, Isaiah had prophesied that a virgin would bring forth the Messiah (Isaiah 7:14). The time had finally come for that word to be fulfilled.

Mary was that virgin, and she said, "My soul magnifies the Lord, and my spirit has rejoiced in God my Savior. For He has regarded the lowly state of His maidservant; for behold, henceforth all generations will call me blessed" (Luke 1:46-48). God chose an ordinary young woman to birth a King who would come from the tribe of celebration and praise "to give light to those who sit in darkness and the shadow of death, to guide our feet into the way of peace" (Luke 1:79).

Thousands of people thronged Bethlehem at the time of Jesus' birth. They did not notice that their Savior was born; like Joseph and Mary, they were in town for the census registration and tax collection decreed by Caesar Augustus. But the Savior's birth did not go unnoticed. God chose certain ones to come to the celebration.

Those Who Celebrated His Birth

On the dark Judean hillside, shepherds were watching over their flocks when an angel of the Lord suddenly stood before them (Luke 2:8-9). I do not know why the Lord chose shepherds to celebrate the birth of Christ. I would like to think that it was because Jesus is both the great Shepherd (Hebrews 13:20) and the Lamb of God who took away the sin of the world (John 1:29). These lowly shepherds came to celebrate the birth of the great Shepherd. No doubt these shepherds raised sheep to be sold for sacrificing; they worshiped the Lamb who would be sacrificed for their sins and the sins of the whole world.

The shepherds were afraid of the angel, but the angel said, "Do not be afraid, for behold, I bring you good tidings of great joy which will be to all people. For there is born to you this day in the city of David a Savior, who is Christ the Lord" (Luke 2:10-11). This was good news, and it called for an angelic celebration! The Savior was born, and His birth would benefit all people. The heavenly host praised God: "Glory to God in the highest, and on earth

repentance to Life

peace, goodwill toward men!" The God of glory brought salvation to mankind; He was called Immanuel, God with us. He deserved to be celebrated. The arm of the Lord had been revealed (Isaiah 53:1). God's peace and goodwill belonged especially to those who welcomed and celebrated God's only Son. This was a celebration time then, and it is just as much now.

The angel had told the shepherds they would find the newborn Savior in the city of David (Bethlehem). He would be lying in a manger, wrapped in swaddling clothes. They left the hillside and hurried into town, searching through the avenues and side streets. When they saw the infant Savior with their own eyes, they excitedly told Mary and Joseph about the angelic choir. They spread the story throughout the town, but Mary pondered in her heart the angelic visits, her child's birth, and the shepherds' adoration. The shepherds went away glorifying and praising God because the things they had heard and seen were just as the angel said they would be.

Simeon was another celebrant of the birth of the Savior. Simeon had waited a long time for the consolation of Israel (Luke 2:25-26), the Comforter, the Messiah, the One who would bring salvation to the Jew and the Gentile. The Holy Spirit had revealed to Simeon that he would not die until he had seen the salvation of God. When he saw Joseph and Mary walking into the court of the Temple with the baby, Simeon, prompted by the Holy Spirit, took the baby in his arms. His declaration, "My eyes have seen Your salvation" (Luke 2:30), revealed that Spirit-taught Simeon knew the identity of this Child. He identified God's salvation as being personified in Jesus!

Joseph and Mary were still amazed at their encounter with Simeon when an ancient widow lady named Anna approached and recognized Jesus as the Redeemer. She was a constant and devout worshiper who fasted often, praying for the Messiah to come. Excited and joyful, she spread the news throughout Jerusalem (Luke 2:36-38).

The Redeemer had come to mankind! *Redemption* means "to ransom, to redeem, something to loosen with, which is a redemption price."[2] Peter wrote, "You were not redeemed with corruptible things, like silver and gold, from your aimless conduct received by tradition from your fathers, but with the precious blood of Christ, as of a lamb without blemish and without spot" (I Peter 1:18-19).

The celebration did not end with Anna. Several months (or as long as two years) after Jesus' birth, wise men from the East knocked on Joseph and Mary's door, asking to see the young child so they could worship Him and give Him gifts (Matthew 2:11). It is a mystery how these Gentiles knew that the star indicated that the King of the Jews had been born or why they traveled so far to a foreign land to worship a foreign king. Perhaps thousands of others saw the star and it meant nothing to them, but it spoke volumes to these men. They responded to this special birth with belief, obedience, and self-sacrifice. When the wise men found Jesus, they worshiped Him, rejoicing with exceedingly great joy (Matthew 2:9-10).

Those who were the most acquainted with the Word of God—the learned priests, scribes, and lawyers these were not called to the celebration. Neither were the rich and famous such as Annas, Caiaphas, King Herod, or Pontius Pilate. No, God chose a handful of lowly shepherds, two well-seasoned saints, and some foreign wise men to rejoice at His Son's birth and to spread the word.

All of these celebrants teach us that God speaks to us in a language we can understand. A person's race, age, gender, education, or socioeconomic status does not matter; sooner or later, God has a word, a song, or a star for each one. This miraculous birth affected mankind from the least to the greatest, and it is still affecting lives today. People are still celebrating the King!

chapter two

Celebrating Christ's Death

god's plan and purpose for the Messiah's life were for the salvation of mankind. "Surely he has borne our griefs, and carried our sorrows; yet we esteemed Him stricken, smitten by God, and afflicted. . . . Yet it pleased the LORD to bruise Him; He has put Him to grief. When You make His soul an offering for sin, He shall see His seed, He shall prolong his days, and the pleasure of the LORD shall prosper in his hand. He shall see the labor of His soul, and be satisfied" (Isaiah 53:4, 10-11).

The omnipresent Spirit of God took on flesh. "*'Behold, the virgin shall be with child, and bear a Son, and they shall call His name Immanuel,'* which is translated, 'God with us' " (Matthew 1:23). "God was in Christ reconciling the world to Himself, not imputing their trespasses to them, and has committed to us the word of reconciliation" (II Corinthians 5:19). God reconciled the world to Himself through the death of the man Christ Jesus. Christ died in our place and for our sin. When we are born again, God counts Jesus' righteousness as our righteousness.

The "word of reconciliation" that has been entrusted to us who have been born again is to tell people that God wants to restore them to a relationship with Himself. We are messengers or ambassadors for Christ. It is as though God is pleading through us for others to be reconciled to Him. The sacrifice of Jesus makes this possible.

God foreordained Jesus Christ to effect reconciliation with mankind. Because He loved us, God wanted to be our Savior, so He gave Himself for us. It took the sacrifice of a Lamb without spot or blemish. Not just any man would do, because all the men on earth were full of sin and needed to be saved. It took a man who knew no sin to become sin for us.

Jesus was born to reconcile us to God, and He did that through His flesh and blood. "And I will pour on the house of David and on the inhabitants of Jerusalem the Spirit of grace and supplication; then they will look on Me whom they pierced" (Zechariah 12:10). "And without controversy great is the mystery of godliness: God was manifested in the flesh" (I Timothy 3:16). There is no dispute; the mystery has been solved. God was manifested in the flesh because He loved us, and His flesh was pierced for us. "For God so loved the world that He gave His only begotten Son" (John 3:16). With His own right arm God brought salvation; no one else could do it (Isaiah 59:16).

When Jesus asked John to baptize Him and Jesus came up out of the water, the heavens opened and the Spirit of God descended like a dove upon Jesus. A voice from heaven said, "This is My beloved Son, in whom I am well pleased" (Matthew 3:17). God was pleased with His Son because of what Jesus was going to accomplish for Him. He was the Lamb of God, and He would take away the sins of the world (John 1:29). In Isaiah 53:11, Jesus was the Servant of God: "By His knowledge My righteous Servant shall justify many, for He shall bear their iniquities." The victory wrought by Jesus' death caused heaven to celebrate.

When John the Baptist was still in his mother's womb, he leaped for joy when he heard Mary's greeting. Elizabeth said to Mary, "Blessed is the fruit of your womb!" (Luke 1:42). John rejoiced in his mother's womb because of the coming of Jesus. John was sent to bear witness of the Light, that Light being Jesus (John 1:6-7). When John saw Jesus coming toward him he said, "Behold! The Lamb of God, who takes away the sin of the world!" (John 1:29). John preached about the One who would come, and when he saw Jesus, he rejoiced because this man was the sacrificial Lamb.

In Revelation, the Lamb was exalted:

> Now when He had taken the scroll, the four living creatures and the twenty-four elders fell down before the Lamb, each having a harp, and golden bowls full of incense, which are the prayers of the saints. And they sang a new song, saying:
>
> "You are worthy to take the scroll, and to open its seals;
> For You were slain, and have redeemed us to God by Your blood
> Out of every tribe and tongue and people and nation,
> And have made us kings and priests to our God;
> And we shall reign on the earth."
>
> Then I looked, and I heard the voice of many angels around the throne, the living creatures, and the elders; and the number of them was ten thousand times ten thousand, and thousands of thousands, saying with a loud voice:
>
> "Worthy is the Lamb who was slain
> To receive power and riches and wisdom,
> And strength and honor and glory and blessing!"
>
> And every creature which is in heaven and on the earth and under the earth and such as are in the sea, and all that are in them, I heard saying:

repentance to Life

> "Blessing and honor and glory and power
> Be to Him who sits on the throne,
> And to the Lamb, forever and ever!"
>
> Then the four living creatures said, "Amen!" And the twenty-four elders fell down and worshiped Him who lives forever and ever (Revelation 5:8-14).

Jesus Christ is to be exalted for His sacrifice on the cross, for redeeming us, or "buying us back" to God. In ancient times, one could buy back a person who was sold into slavery. In the same way, Christ through His death bought us from our slavery to sin (Ephesians 1:7).[3] Our sin separated us from Him. Paul wrote about the redemption we have in Christ: "Blessed be the God and Father of our Lord Jesus Christ, who has blessed us with every spiritual blessing in the heavenly places in Christ, just as He chose us in Him before the foundation of the world, that we should be holy and without blame before Him in love, having predestined us to adoption as sons by Jesus Christ to Himself, according to the good pleasure of His will, to the praise of the glory of His grace, by which He made us accepted in the Beloved" (Ephesians 1:3-6).[4]

Before the world was created, God chose His church in Jesus Christ to be holy and without blame. He foreordained His church to be adopted by Jesus Christ. "Therefore you are no longer a slave but a son, and if a son, then an heir of God through Christ" (Galatians 4:7). Paul said, "In Him we have redemption through His blood, the forgiveness of sins, according to the riches of His grace" (Ephesians 1:7). (See Colossians 1:14.) Jesus Christ was the Lamb slain from the foundation of the world (Revelation 13:8) because without shedding of blood there was no remission of sins (Hebrews 9:22).

It was God's idea and plan before the world began that Jesus would be slain, we would be forgiven, and we would be called the sons of God. Jesus' death on the cross was a glorious time in the eyes of God because His human creation would be redeemed with the precious blood of Christ. (See I Peter 1:18-19.)

chapter three

Celebrating Christ's Resurrection

Celebrating Christ's Resurrection

God's plan for Jesus was not to leave His body in the grave but to triumph over it. David prophesied, "You will not abandon me to the grave, nor will you let your Holy One see decay" (Psalm 16:10, NIV). God celebrated Christ's victory over the grave. David also celebrated in that victory, for he said, "Therefore my heart is glad and my tongue rejoices; my body also will rest secure" (Psalm 16:9, NIV). Now you and I, because of Christ's triumph, will also have that same victory over the grave.

Jesus Christ was the first one to conquer death. "But Christ has indeed been raised from the dead, the firstfruits of those who have fallen asleep. For since death came through a man, the resurrection of the dead comes also through a man. For as in Adam all die, so in Christ all will be made alive" (I Corinthians 15:20-22, NIV). If Jesus had not overcome death, then you and I would not be able to either. (See I Corinthians 15:12-18.)

"I am He who lives, and was dead, and behold, I am alive forevermore. Amen. And I have the keys of Hades and of Death" (Revelation 1:18). Jesus unlocked the door of death for you and me. God gave us the victory through Jesus Christ. "So when this corruptible has put on incorruption, and this mortal has put on immortality, then shall be brought to pass the saying that is written: *'Death is swallowed up in victory.' 'O Death, where is your sting? O Hades, where is your victory?'* The sting of death is sin, and the strength of sin is the law. But thanks be to God, who gives us the victory through our Lord Jesus Christ" (I Corinthians 15:54-57).

God, in His mercy and love for us, celebrated Christ's coming to this earth for the redemption of mankind. Through Jesus' death, burial, and resurrection, God was celebrated as Savior, giving us the victory over sin. "He indeed was foreordained before the foundation of the world, but was manifest in these last times for you who through Him believe in God, who raised Him from the dead and gave Him glory, so that your faith and hope are in God" (I Peter 1:20-21).

The Coming of the Holy Spirit

The coming of the Holy Spirit was also a time of great celebration. The plan in the mind of God before the foundation of the world was for us, through Jesus Christ, to be sealed with the promised Holy Spirit.

God used Jesus Christ to redeem mankind from sin, to give us hope of salvation. We, like Jesus who arose from the dead, can also through Jesus Christ have that same hope of resurrection by His Spirit who is in us.

God's plan was to pour out His Spirit on all flesh, as the angel of the Lord told the shepherds, "I bring you good tidings of great joy which will be to all people." The birth of Jesus was a good thing for all people, and so was the coming of the Spirit. It was our hope of glory. John the Baptist spoke of the Holy Spirit. John was a witness of the Light (John 1:7.) He would testify of the Light. He preached to the people that One mightier than he was coming who would baptize them with the Holy Spirit.

John said, "I saw the Spirit descending from heaven like a dove, and He remained upon Him. . . . 'Upon whom you see the Spirit descending, and remaining on Him, this is He who baptizes with the Holy Spirit.' And I have seen and testified that this is the

Son of God" (John 1:32-34). John witnessed the Light, the Son of God, the One who would baptize with the Holy Spirit. Jesus would fulfill the Old Testament prophecies concerning the outpouring of the Spirit on mankind.

Jesus talked about the Spirit at different times, telling the believers that it was coming. Jesus was the One who would be responsible for this great celebration of the Spirit. In John 3, Jesus told Nicodemus that he must be born of the water and of the Spirit. In John 4, Jesus told the Samaritan woman about the Living Water: "Whoever drinks of the water that I shall give him will never thirst. But the water that I shall give him will become in him a fountain of water springing up into everlasting life" (John 4:14). Jesus said He would give us this Living Water. Jesus stood and cried, "'If anyone thirsts, let him come to Me and drink. He who believes in Me, as the Scripture has said, out of his heart will flow rivers of living water.' But this He spoke concerning the Spirit, whom those believing in Him would receive" (John 7:37-39).

The living water was the Holy Spirit. Just as it was important for certain ones to celebrate Jesus' birth, it was important for John to identify the Holy Spirit baptizer and for us to know and celebrate the Spirit in our lives.

As the disciples ate the Last Supper with Jesus, they did not have a clue about what was going to happen to Jesus. Jesus talked to them about the Holy Spirit, a subject they did not yet understand. But it was important for them to know about this, for they would be witnesses of the Holy Spirit in their own lives and in the lives of others. Jesus said, "If you love Me, keep My commandments. And I will pray the Father, and He will give you another Helper [Comforter], that He may abide with you forever" (John 14:15-16). As long as Jesus was with the disciples they were comforted, but Jesus knew that He would soon be leaving them. He

repentance to Life

also knew what was going to happen to these men and how they were going to react to his death. (See John 16:32-33.)

Jesus was giving the disciples some hope, even though they did not realize the import of His words. In John 17, Jesus prayed for Himself, because the hour had come for the Lamb to be slain. Then He prayed that the disciples would be preserved, and not only the disciples but also those who would believe through their words. Jesus prayed that they would receive a Comforter who would abide with them forever. It was humanity praying to deity. "The Spirit of truth, whom the world cannot receive, because it neither sees Him nor knows Him; but you know Him, for He dwells with you and will be in you. I will not leave you orphans; I will come to you. . . . But the Helper, the Holy Spirit, whom the Father will send in My name, He will teach you all things" (John 14:17-18, 26).

Jesus explained that the Comforter was the Holy Spirit. The apostle John wrote of Jesus' words: "But this He spoke concerning the Spirit, whom those believing in Him would receive; for the Holy Spirit was not yet given, because Jesus was not yet glorified" (John 7:39). Jesus told the believers that He was the Comforter, the Holy Spirit, who was with them right then but that soon after He went away and was glorified, He would come back to dwell in them.

Jesus told the disciples, "It is to your advantage that I go away; for if I do not go away, the Helper will not come to you; but if I depart, I will send Him to you" (John 16:7). In the same way, if Jesus had not come to earth, died, resurrected, and ascended, we would not be able to receive Spirit baptism and would not have hope of a resurrection. Jesus had to come, offer Himself as a sacrifice, rise from the dead, and go away so we could receive all the promises of salvation. Because of Jesus Christ we can celebrate the Holy Spirit in our lives, for it is Christ in us, the hope of glory (Colossians 1:27).

"Exalted to the right hand of God, he has received from the Father the promised Holy Spirit and has poured out what you now see and hear" (Acts 2:33, NIV). Jesus, through His death, burial, and resurrection, was exalted and given all power and authority. Because He went away, He sent back the Comforter to live in us so we could celebrate Jesus in our lives as Lord and Savior.

Every soul must have the Spirit of Christ to make it to heaven. "And if anyone does not have the Spirit of Christ, he does not belong to Christ. . . . And if the Spirit of him who raised Jesus from the dead is living in you, he who raised Christ from the dead will also give life to your mortal bodies through his Spirit, who lives in you" (Romans 8:9, 11, NIV). (See John 2:19-22.)

What about the children of God, the holy men of old, who died previous to the coming of the Spirit? They, too, have a hope that their souls will not be left in the grave because of the prophecies that spoke of the coming Savior. (See Psalm 16:9-10.) "I do not want you to be ignorant, brethren, concerning those who have fallen asleep, lest you sorrow as others who have no hope. For if we believe that Jesus died and rose again, even so God will bring with Him those who sleep in Jesus. . . . And the dead in Christ will rise first" (I Thessalonians 4:13-14, 16). Without the resurrecting power of Christ, no one will rise; that is why it so important for us to have His Spirit within us.

"You believe in him and are filled with an inexpressible and glorious joy, for you are receiving the goal of your faith, the salvation of your souls. Concerning this salvation, the prophets, who spoke of the grace that was to come to you, searched intently and with the greatest care, trying to find out the time and circumstances to which the Spirit of Christ in them was pointing when he predicted the sufferings of Christ and the glories that would follow. It was revealed to them that they were not serving themselves but you, when they spoke of the things that

repentance to Life

have now been told you by those who have preached the gospel to you by the Holy Spirit sent from heaven" (I Peter 1:8-12, NIV). The prophets of old were moved on by the Spirit of God to write concerning the sufferings of Jesus, and that same Spirit was sent into our lives to save us and to help us preach the gospel of Christ to others.

The Comforter, who is the Holy Spirit, was sent down from heaven to be celebrated in our lives as our intercessor, consoler, and advocate. An intercessor is someone who comes between, asking earnestly, pleading a request or petition on another's behalf. "He saw that there was no man, and wondered that there was no intercessor; therefore His own arm brought salvation for Him; and His own righteousness, it sustained Him" (Isaiah 59:16).

God heard our cry and acted in behalf of our need, just as He did when He saved the children of Israel from Egyptian bondage. "Behold, God is my salvation, I will trust and not be afraid; for YAH, the LORD, is my strength and song; He also has become my salvation" (Isaiah 12:2). *Jehovah* means "self-existent, eternal, the Lord God." *Salvation* means "to deliver, save, set free, rescue."[5] The self-existent God became our deliverer and our Savior. No one else could do this. " 'You are My witnesses,' says the LORD, 'and My servant whom I have chosen, that you may know and believe Me, and understand that I am He. Before Me there was no God formed, nor shall there be after Me. I, even I, am the LORD, and besides Me there is no savior' " (Isaiah 43:10-11).

Consoler means "to alleviate or lessen the grief, sorrow, or disappointment of; give solace or comfort."[6] God gave His only begotten Son to save humanity. "Who has believed our report? And to whom has the arm of the LORD been revealed?" (Isaiah 53:1). God's arm brought salvation because there was no other intercessor. Our intercessor has come. "And he bore the sin of many, and made intercession for the transgressors" (Isaiah 53:12).

Advocate means "a person who pleads for or in behalf of another; intercessor."[7] "If anyone sins, we have an Advocate with the Father, Jesus Christ the righteous. And He Himself is the propitiation for our sins, and not for ours only but also for the whole world" (I John 2:1-2). Jesus Christ is our intercessor and our advocate. He also is our consoler, for He bore our grief and carried our sorrows. God became our salvation when He was manifested in Christ.

Jesus Christ is our Comforter, which is the Holy Spirit. When we are born again, we are reconciled back to God. God accepts us because Jesus is the advocate between God and us. When we turn our hearts toward God, God accepts us because of Jesus Christ. "In this the love of God was manifested toward us, that God has sent His only begotten Son into the world, that we might live through Him. In this is love, not that we loved God, but that He loved us and sent His Son to be the propitiation for our sins" (I John 4:9-10).

We celebrate the Holy Spirit in our lives because Jesus reconciled us back to God by His Spirit. "Now he who keeps His commandments abides in Him, and He in him. And by this we know that He abides in us, by the Spirit whom He has given us" (I John 3:24).

God celebrates the Spirit of Christ in us as the way of reconciling us back to Him. "For it is the God who commanded light to shine out of darkness, who has shone in our hearts to give the light of the knowledge of the glory of God in the face of Jesus Christ" (II Corinthians 4:6).

chapter four

The Godhead

The Father

"**Now the birth** of Jesus Christ was as follows: After His mother Mary was betrothed to Joseph, before they came together, she was found with child of the Holy Spirit. . . . 'For that which is conceived in her is of the Holy Spirit'" (Matthew 1:18, 20). "He will be great, and will be called the Son of the Highest; and the Lord God will give Him the throne of His father David. . . . The Holy Spirit will come upon you [Mary], . . . therefore, also, that Holy One who is to be born will be called the Son of God" (Luke 1:32, 35).

The Holy Spirit caused Mary to conceive; therefore, the Holy Spirit was the Father. Jesus was the Son of the Highest. *Holy Spirit* means "a current of air, breath, or breeze; God, or Christ's Spirit." The *Highest* means "the Supreme (God)."[8] God overshadowed Mary, and she conceived the Messiah.

God is the all-powerful living Spirit. The psalmist wrote of gods that were dead. "But our God is in heaven; He does whatever He pleases. Their idols are silver and gold, the work of men's hands. They have mouths, but they do not speak; eyes they have, but they do not see; they have ears, but they do not hear; noses they have, but they do not smell; they have hands, but they do not handle; feet they have, but they do not walk; nor do they mutter through their throat" (Psalm 115:3-7). These man-made gods were dead and worthless. They had no life, no spirit. A spirit is a breath of inspiration, a principle that pervades thought and stirs one to action. These gods had no life and no spirit and therefore could not act or inspire others to act.

God is a Spirit, alive and full of action. He sees, hears, speaks, moves, and creates. He fills the universe. He has no limitations. God's Spirit moved upon the face of the waters. He created the heavens and the earth (Genesis 1:1-2). God is the only Father. "You, O LORD, are our Father; our Redeemer from Everlasting is Your name" (Isaiah 63:16). "But now, O LORD, You are our Father; we are the clay, and You our potter; and all we are the work of Your hand" (Isaiah 64:8). (See John 8:41; Ephesians 4:6.)

God was the Father of all (Ephesians 4:6), who spoke the world into existence. He moved upon Mary, causing her to conceive and bear a son. Jesus was the only being God created in this fashion. God and Mary were the parents of this Holy One. The man Christ Jesus was subject to His Father (the Holy Spirit) and was His servant (Isaiah 42:1). He was obedient to the will of God and His purpose.

God was the Father of creation, the Creator of life and all living things. No one else could take the credit or the glory for what our Father did. The Holy Spirit of God, who spoke the world into existence, breathed into Adam the breath of life, and overshadowed Mary, is the same Spirit or Father who breathes new life into us when we are born of the Spirit.

Until God breathed into Adam the breath of life, Adam was lifeless. Unless we have been born of the Spirit, we are physically alive but spiritually dead in trespasses and sin. In John 3, Jesus told Nicodemus he needed to be born again. Likewise, we who have been born of the flesh need to be born of the Spirit. We must be born again because we, unlike Jesus, had an earthly father and were born with a lower nature full of trespasses and sins. Being born again means being born of the Spirit. The Spirit of God, who is sinless, becomes our Father.

Jesus told Nicodemus, " 'I tell you the truth, no one can see the kingdom of God unless he is born again.' 'How can a man be born when he is old?' Nicodemus asked. 'Surely he cannot enter a second time into his mother's womb to be born!' " (John 3:3-4, NIV). Some suggest that when Jesus told Nicodemus he had to be born of the water, He was referring to Nicodemus's natural birth. However, Nicodemus had obviously already been born, so why would Jesus tell the elderly Jewish ruler that he first had to be born of his mother? That was certainly not the issue here. The issue was that Nicodemus—and everyone else—had to be born again. Jesus did not mean that a man had to enter again into his mother's womb, but that he had to be born from above. "For you have been born again, not of perishable seed, but of imperishable, through the living and enduring word of God" (I Peter 1:23, NIV). We who have been born again were born from the non-decaying, always living, everlasting Word of God.

When we are born again, we are born of the Spirit. The Spirit is our Father. When we are born of the water and the Spirit we become a new creature, a new person. (See II Corinthians 5:17; Titus 3:5.) Because we are born again, the Father abides in us and we in Him (I John 4:13). "I will sprinkle clean water on you, and you shall be clean. . . . I will give you a new heart and put a new spirit within you" (Ezekiel 36:25-26). "And it shall come to pass afterward that I will pour out My Spirit on all flesh" (Joel 2:28). On the Day of Pentecost, they were all filled with the Holy Spirit and water baptized in Jesus' name (Acts 2). They were born again of the water and the Spirit. The Father put His Spirit within them, and they became sons of God. When we are born again, we have a familial connection with God; we take on our Father's name in baptism. The Father's name, which is Jesus, is above all names. (See Acts 4:12.)

repentance to Life

In John 13-16, Jesus was in deep discussion with the disciples. In John 14:1-14, Jesus was preparing the disciples because He knew they would be bewildered by His death and did not want them to be troubled by the imminent traumatic events; He wanted them to trust in Him. He explained that He was going to prepare a place for them and He would come back to take them there to live with Him forever. Jesus said they knew the way to where He was going. Thomas said, "'Lord, we do not know where You are going, and how can we know the way?' Jesus said to him, 'I am the way, the truth, and the life. No one comes to the Father except through Me. If you had known Me, you would have known My Father also; and from now on you know Him and have seen Him'" (John 14:5-7).

Jesus often spoke of His Father. The Jews thought of God as their Father, but Jesus said that if they really knew Him (Jesus) they would have known the Father also. He had taught the disciples by word and example for three and one-half years, yet some of them still did not understand that He was God manifested in flesh. The disciples had seen Jesus' mother, but they did not understand that they also had "seen" His Father because they had seen Jesus. The problem was that as yet they truly did not know Jesus Christ. Jesus told them that from then on they knew the Father and had seen Him.

Jesus not only referred to His Father but often prayed to Him. It was humanity praying to deity. Philip said, "Lord, show us the Father, and it is sufficient for us" (John 14:8). Philip did not expect this answer from Jesus: "Have I been with you so long, and yet you have not known Me, Philip? He who has seen Me has seen the Father; so how can you say, 'Show us the Father'?" (John 14:9).

When Jesus said, "He who has seen Me has seen the Father," He was showing the disciples His divine nature, which they did not understand until later. This same answer applies to us. When we truly know who Jesus is, we will know who the Father is also. When we were born from above, we "saw" Him and knew Him. In baptism, we took on our Father's name; we knew who our Father was.

Jesus was Immanuel, God with us (Matthew 1:23). God had walked and talked with the disciples all this time, but they had not looked at Jesus as being God in all His fullness. They stumbled over the humanity of Jesus. Jesus was just as human as they were, but at the same time He was God. They sensed that Jesus was different because He performed miracles and taught with unprecedented authority. However, if they truly had known who Jesus was, they would not have asked Jesus to show them the Father. The truth is that everything God is, Jesus claimed to be. Jesus was God manifested in flesh.

"Do you not believe that I am in the Father, and the Father in Me? The words that I speak to you I do not speak on My own authority; but the Father who dwells in Me does the works" (John 14:10). Jesus was the temple that was created for God to do His work. (See Hebrews 10:5-7.) Before the world was created, the Incarnation was in the mind and plan of God. God could have chosen another way to do this, but He chose this way. God was reconciling the world unto Himself through Jesus Christ.

Jesus' purpose was like no other. His purpose was to be our Savior: a sinless human sacrifice, a Lamb without spot or blemish. He was the image of the invisible God, the embodiment of all of God's attributes. That's why Jesus could say, "He who has seen Me has seen the Father." Jesus spoke with divine authority and power; He performed all the miracles by His Father's power. Jesus told the disciples, "Believe me when I say that I am in the Father and the Father is in me; or at least believe on the evidence of the miracles themselves" (John 14:11, NIV). (See John 10:38.)

Jesus was one with His Father. He cried, "He who believes in Me, believes not in Me but in Him who sent Me. And he who sees

Me sees Him who sent Me" (John 12:44-45). God sent his Son into the world that the world through Him might be saved. (See John 3:17.) When we see Jesus, we see Jehovah, the Creator, the Savior. (Compare with Acts 9:5.) God commanded the light to shine out of darkness, and the darkness could not overcome it. The Word that was with God—and was God—became flesh and came into a dark world to give light to all men.

"And the Word became flesh and dwelt among us, and we beheld His glory, the glory as of the only begotten of the Father, full of grace and truth" (John 1:14). "For it is the God who commanded light to shine out of darkness, who has shone in our hearts to give the light of the knowledge of the glory of God in the face of Jesus Christ" (II Corinthians 4:6). When the men of that day saw Jesus' face, they saw the Father. Jesus was the Word made flesh, the Incarnation.

We celebrate Jesus Christ as the Father in creation (John 1:3, 10) and when we are born again (John 3:5; Acts 4:12). "When the fullness of the time had come, God sent forth His Son, born of a woman, born under the law, to redeem those who were under the law, that we might receive the adoption as sons. And because you are sons, God has sent forth the Spirit of His Son into your hearts, crying out, 'Abba, Father!'" (Galatians 4:4-6). (See John 14:18.)

"He Who Believes in Me, As the Scripture Has Said"

Considering what Jesus did for us, it is hard to comprehend the magnitude of the gift that we have been given. It is also hard to comprehend why God did this. The only motivation that would be great enough was His love for us.

"You shall call His name JESUS." *Name* means "a word or phrase by which a person or thing is designated. An appellation as a mark, or memorial of individuality; by implication, honor, authority, or character."[9] *Appellation* means "identifying name, title, or designation."[10] *Individuality* means "a particular character, or aggregate of qualities, that distinguishes one person or thing from others."[11] *Called* means "to name or address (someone) as to designate as something specified."[12]

The child whose birth fulfilled Old Testament prophecy was not given a name like John or Mark, but his name denoted qualities, characteristics, or designations. Isaiah prophesied that a virgin would conceive and bear a son and would call His name Immanuel (Isaiah 7:14). Matthew wrote that *Immanuel* means "God with us." This Son's name, Immanuel, was a title or mark; it was a way of revealing what and who this child was.

This Son was not an "average" human being whose mother named Him what she thought was a nice name and what she hoped He would become like. As the angel had told her, Mary named Him Immanuel, "God with us." We can believe in Him as God. We can identify Him by His name in our own lives. "As many as received Him, to them He gave the right to become children of God, to those who believe in His name" (John 1:12). "As Moses lifted up the serpent in the wilderness, even so must the Son of Man be lifted up, that whoever believes in Him should not perish but have eternal life. . . . He who believes in Him is not condemned; but he who does not believe is condemned already, because he has not believed in the name of the only begotten Son of God" (John 3:14-15, 18). *Believe* means "to convince, persuade, give credence, have faith (in, upon, or with respect to, a person or thing)."[13] When we believe in the name of the only begotten Son of God, we believe in who He is. We believe in Him as the Scriptures have said.

In John 4, the woman at the well thought Jesus was a prophet because He told her about the things she had done. This was a fair assumption on her part because prophets were used in that way. However, Jesus indicated to this woman the name by which He was "designated"—Messiah. The woman said, "'I know that Messiah is coming' (who is called Christ). 'When He comes, He will tell us all things.' Jesus said to her, 'I who speak to you am He'" (John 4:25-26). Jesus identified Himself as the One for whom she waited. The "child" who was given, now stood before her as the Messiah, the Christ.

Even after thousands of years the reality of His love, sacrifice, and provision for us still rings true. In understanding Jesus Christ, Isaiah 9:6 has become my favorite verse of Scripture: "For unto us a Child is born, unto us a Son is given; and the government will be upon His shoulder. And His name will be called Wonderful, Counselor, Mighty God, Everlasting Father, Prince of Peace" (Isaiah 9:6). We have been given a child, a Son. This could be said of only one person in all the earth: Jesus Christ. There was no other reason for His birth except as a sinless sacrifice for the remission of our sins.

In order to believe on Jesus "as the Scripture has said," we need to understand who Jesus is. Let us look at some of Jesus' statements and some made about Him. "He who believes in Me, as the Scripture has said. . ." (John 7:38). Jesus longed for people to believe on Him. Jesus spent time teaching His disciples and the people about Himself. He was the Messiah, the Savior. Jesus said, "For God so loved the world that He gave His only begotten Son" (John 3:16). This was the fulfillment of a promise God had made during the time of Adam and Eve. "And I will put enmity between you and the woman, and between your offspring and hers; he will crush your head, and you will strike his heel" (Genesis 3:15, NIV). Jesus was the woman's offspring who would destroy Satan. Satan's blow hurt Jesus for a short time, but Jesus will destroy Satan for eternity. Satan no longer has a stranglehold on us, because Jesus overcame death, hell, and the grave. Sin can no longer rule over the children of God.

"There shall come forth a Rod from the stem of Jesse, and a Branch shall grow out of his roots. The Spirit of the LORD shall rest upon Him, the Spirit of wisdom and understanding, the Spirit of counsel and might, the Spirit of knowledge and of the fear of the LORD" (Isaiah 11:1-2). Jesus was David's offspring. Jesus would be the King of kings, and the Spirit of God would be in Him. The arm of the Lord would be revealed. "For He shall grow up before Him as a tender plant, and as a root out of dry ground. He has no form or comeliness; and when we see Him, there is no beauty that we should desire Him" (Isaiah 53:2). Rather than in physical beauty, Jesus Christ's comeliness manifested itself in majesty, holiness, righteousness, and the glory of God.

"And in that day there shall be a Root of Jesse, who shall stand as a banner to the people; for the Gentiles shall seek Him, and His resting place shall be glorious" (Isaiah 11:10). Every nation that seeks Jesus will find glorious hope. The Lord told Abraham that in him all families of the earth should be blessed (Genesis 12:3). Jesus gave all nations the opportunity to be of the seed of Abraham through salvation. (See Matthew 28:19-20; Acts 2:38.)

Isaiah 9:6 offers special insight into the nature and person of Jesus Christ. In this study we have already addressed the fact that Jesus was the child, the Son, who fulfilled Isaiah's prophecy. Next we will show how Jesus fulfilled each of the designations Isaiah ascribed to Him: Ruler, Wonderful Counselor, Mighty God, Everlasting Father, Prince of Peace.

"The government will be upon His shoulder" (Isaiah 9:6). Upon this Son was supreme power in governing. He was sovereign. "But you, Bethlehem Ephrathah, though you are little among the thousands of Judah, yet out of you shall come forth to Me the One to be Ruler in Israel, whose goings forth are from of old, from everlasting" (Micah 5:2; Matthew 2:6). We have been given a leader, a prince, and a ruler. "Of the increase of His government and peace there will be no end, upon the throne of David and over His kingdom, to order it and establish it with judgment and justice from that time forward, even forever. The zeal of the LORD of hosts will perform this" (Isaiah 9:7).

In the Old Testament, the children of Israel wanted to be ruled by a king like other nations. Their request displeased Samuel, who went to God with this matter. God told Samuel to give the children of Israel what they wanted. The people had not rejected Samuel, but they had rejected God. In spite of the warning against it, Israel persisted in this request. They wanted a human king to judge them, to go out before them, and to fight their battles (I Samuel 8.) They were not satisfied with a theocracy, even though God had delivered them from Egypt, provided for them in the wilderness, and fought for them as they entered the Promised Land. Instead of the all-powerful King of kings, they settled for a human king full of faults and limitations, who let the power of his position go to his head.

David wrote concerning the King of kings: "Who is this King of glory? The LORD strong and mighty, the LORD mighty in battle. . . . Who is this King of glory? The LORD of hosts, He is the King of glory" (Psalm 24:8, 10). God said, "I am the LORD, your Holy One, the Creator of Israel, your King" (Isaiah 43:15). The God of Israel was the King of kings (Isaiah 6:1-5).

When Jesus was born in Bethlehem, Israel was given a King: "Out of you shall come forth to Me the One to be Ruler in Israel" (Micah 5:2). Because they had seen His star in the East, wise men journeyed to Jerusalem, looking for the newborn King of the Jews. They came to worship Him. But Israel again rejected the King of kings and demanded that He be crucified. Even though they hated Rome, they told Pilate that they preferred Rome's emperor to their own King. "Now it was the Preparation Day of the Passover, and about the sixth hour. And he [Pilate] said to the Jews, 'Behold your King!' But they cried out, 'Away with Him, away with Him! Crucify Him!' Pilate said to them, 'Shall I crucify your King?' The chief priests answered, 'We have no king but Caesar!'" (John 19:14-15).

The Jewish leaders could not kill the King of kings; He was from old, from everlasting. His kingdom had no end. They did not understand that they were fulfilling Old Testament prophecy when they crucified the Lamb of God during the very feast in which they performed the ancient ritual of slaying the Passover lamb. If they had believed in the One who gave His life for them, Jesus would have reigned as King in their lives.

"Thus says the LORD, the King of Israel, and his Redeemer, the LORD of hosts: I am the First and I am the Last; besides Me there is no God" (Isaiah 44:6). The King of Israel is the only God; there is no one else. However, Jesus made this same claim: "Behold, I am coming quickly, and My reward is with Me, to give to every one according to his work. I am the Alpha and the Omega, the Beginning and the End, the First and the Last" (Revelation 22:12-13). Jesus Christ is the King of glory! The Lord of hosts is His name.

Isaiah 9:6 designated this child as a Wonderful Counselor. *Counselor* means "adviser or guide."[14] During the time I was questioning my faith and studying this passage of Scripture, I asked the Lord, "How are You my Counselor?" I will never forget what the Lord showed me: "But the Helper, the Holy Spirit, whom the Father will send in My name, He will teach you all things, and bring to your remembrance all things that I said to you" (John 14:26). The NIV begins the verse this way: "But the Counselor, the Holy Spirit. . . ." Isaiah said, "His name will be called Wonderful, Counselor." Jesus said that the Father would send the Counselor in His name.

Jesus is the Holy Spirit that we receive when we are born again. "Holy Spirit" is an identifying name or title that Jesus

repentance to Life

possesses. He can claim this because before He was born He was marked with this honor, authority, and character. "However, when He, the Spirit of truth, has come, He will guide you into all truth; for He will not speak on His own authority, but whatever He hears He will speak; and He will tell you things to come" (John 16:13). Jesus said that His words were not His own but the Father's (John 14:24). Jesus said the same thing about the Holy Spirit. Jesus as a man was not separate from God. He did not do and speak what His flesh wanted but what the Spirit, His Father, willed. Now as the Wonderful Counselor He still speaks unto us the Spirit's words.

The Counselor is our guide and advisor. Jesus is with us not as man but as that ever-present Spirit that spoke the world into existence and breathed into us the breath of life. When the Counselor lives within us, He leads and guides us into all truth (John 14:6). "But the anointing which you have received from Him abides in you, and you do not need that anyone teach you; but as the same anointing teaches you concerning all things, and is true, and is not a lie, and just as it has taught you, you will abide in Him" (I John 2:27).

Jesus is our Wonderful Counselor, the creative Spirit, the Word that was in the beginning with God and was God. "No one has seen God at any time. The only begotten Son, who is in the bosom of the Father, He has declared Him" (John 1:18). As a Spirit, God cannot be seen. Yet He can be seen in Jesus, who is the image of that Spirit (Genesis 1:27; Colossians 1:15). "Now to the King eternal, immortal, invisible, to God who alone is wise, be honor and glory forever and ever. Amen" (I Timothy 1:17).

Isaiah said that Jesus Christ was the mighty God (Isaiah 9:6). For centuries the Jews have recited the *Shema Yisrael*, one of the most important sections of the Jewish liturgy. It begins with these words: "Hear, O Israel: The LORD our God, the LORD is one!"

(Deuteronomy 6:4). The passages in Deuteronomy 6:4-9, 11:13-21, and Numbers 15:37-41 taught, among other important precepts, the oneness of God, His love, and the command to instruct one's children in the commandments. Over the centuries the *Shema* became a sort of Jewish "confession of faith."[15] One of the reasons the Jews rejected their Messiah was they did not understand that "their" one almighty God had come in flesh in order to become their Savior. Jesus was the image of this invisible Almighty God. He was Immanuel, God with us. Jesus "declared" or embodied, revealed, and explained this mighty God. Jesus said, "He who believes in Me, believes not in Me but in Him who sent Me. And he who sees Me sees Him who sent Me" (John 12:44-45).

Mighty means "powerful, warrior, chief, and prevailer. Having characteristics of, or showing superior power or strength."[16] *God* means "strength, mighty, the Almighty, the creator and ruler of the universe; the Supreme Being."[17] Jesus Christ is the fleshly image of the only true and living God.

Isaiah prophesied about the "voice of one crying in the wilderness: 'Prepare the way of the LORD; make straight in the desert a highway for our God.' . . . The glory of the LORD shall be revealed, and all flesh shall see it together. . . . O Zion, . . . lift up your voice with strength . . . say to the cities of Judah, 'Behold your God!'" (Isaiah 40:3, 5, 9). John the Baptist was the voice crying in the wilderness. Quoting from Isaiah 40:3 John said, "I am *'The voice of one crying in the wilderness: "Make straight the way of the LORD"'*" (John 1:23). He was sent from God, and he would bear witness of the One who would give light to all men (John 1:6-7). John prepared the way for our God, Jesus Christ. The glory of the Lord was revealed in the man Jesus Christ. (See Isaiah 53.) "And in that day you will say: 'Praise the LORD, call upon His name; declare His deeds among the peoples, make mention that His name is exalted. Sing to the LORD, for He has done excellent things; this is known in all the earth. Cry out and shout, O inhabitant of Zion, for great is the Holy One of Israel in your midst!'" (Isaiah 12:4-6). (See Luke 4:34.)

The arm of the Lord had been revealed. "Break forth into joy, sing together, you waste places of Jerusalem! For the LORD has comforted His people, He has redeemed Jerusalem. The LORD has made bare His holy arm in the eyes of all the nations; and all the ends of the earth shall see the salvation of our God" (Isaiah 52:9-10). Just as a warrior bared his right arm to the shoulder so he could fight unencumbered by battle armor, Jehovah bared His arm in order to reveal His holiness and defeat His foes. In Jesus Christ, the Lord revealed His powerful right arm in order to save His people and deliver them from their enemies. This was unveiled glory, the salvation of our God.[18]

The fact that some do not believe in the arm of the Lord will not stop the Lord from carrying out His will. Jesus will one day rule His people (Matthew 2:6), and "of the increase of his government and peace there will be no end. He will reign on David's throne and over his kingdom, establishing and upholding it with justice and righteousness from that time on and forever. The zeal of the LORD Almighty will accomplish this" (Isaiah 9:7, NIV).

Jesus is a mighty warrior. In Revelation, Jesus (called Faithful and True, the Word of God) will come on a white horse, dressed with a robe dipped in blood. On His robe and thigh will be His name: King of kings and Lord of lords. Out of His mouth will come a sharp sword. In righteousness, He will judge and make war on the nations. (See Revelation 19:11-21.)

"'To whom then will you liken Me, or to whom shall I be equal?' says the Holy One. Lift up your eyes on high, and see who has created these things, who brings out their host by number; He calls them all by name, by the greatness of His might and the strength of His power; not one is missing. . . . Have you not known? Have you not heard? The everlasting God, the LORD, the Creator of the ends of the earth, neither faints nor is weary" (Isaiah 40:25-26, 28).

God has no equal; no one can compare to Him. No one else is as strong in power and might. No one else has His wisdom and knowledge. He is everlasting; He does not get weary or tired. Isaiah wrote, "Thus says the LORD, the King of Israel, and his Redeemer, the LORD of hosts: 'I am the First and I am the Last; besides Me there is no God. . . . Do not fear, nor be afraid; have I not told you from that time, and declared it? You are My witnesses. Is there a God besides Me? Indeed there is no other Rock; I know not one.' . . . Who would form a god or mold an image that profits him nothing? . . . 'I have blotted out, like a thick cloud, your transgressions, and like a cloud, your sins. Return to Me, for I have redeemed you.' Sing, O heavens, for the LORD has done it! Shout, you lower parts of the earth; break forth into singing, you mountains, O forest, and every tree in it! For the LORD has redeemed Jacob, and glorified Himself in Israel. Thus says the LORD, your Redeemer, and He who formed you from the womb: 'I am the LORD, who makes all things, who stretches out the heavens all alone, who spreads abroad the earth by Myself'" (Isaiah 44:6, 8, 10, 22-24).

God is sovereign; He alone is responsible for everything that happens. No human being or graven image can claim this. Jesus is the mighty God, the one true God. He is the image of the invisible God and claimed to be God's equal. "Who, being in the form of God, did not consider it robbery to be equal with God" (Philippians 2:6). Jesus was the only human being who could do this. God asked, "Who is My equal?" The answer is no one, but because He became flesh and dwelled among us, we could see His glory in the "only begotten" of the Father, the man Christ Jesus (John 1:14). Jesus, the man, was equal to God because they were one and the same!

repentance to Life

The Jews wanted to kill Jesus because He claimed that God was His Father, making Himself equal with God (John 5:18). Jesus claimed to be the "I AM" (John 8:58). The Jews recognized this as a claim of eternal existence; they were enraged because Jesus was claiming to be God. They remembered that God had told Moses that His name was "I AM" (Exodus 3:14). Jesus as the mighty God could say this, but not as a man, because His humanity had a beginning. Therefore, the Father was eternally existent but not His flesh, the Son. "In the beginning was the Word, and the Word was with God, and the Word was God. . . . And the Word became flesh and dwelt among us" (John 1:1, 14). The flesh (the Son) had a beginning, and it appeared when Jesus was born in Bethlehem.

The only One who can claim to have been from old, from everlasting, is God. He is eternal. He has no beginning or ending. He is the first and the last. Yet the man Christ Jesus was equal with God. He could claim that same deity, because He was God with us. He is not another God, a lesser God, or a co-equal God; He is the supreme One. It is for this reason Jesus could echo Isaiah 41:4 when He said, "'I am the Alpha and the Omega, the Beginning and the End,' says the Lord, 'who is and who was and who is to come, the Almighty'" (Revelation 1:8).

This mighty God declared that He would not share His glory with another. "I am the LORD, that is My name; and My glory I will not give to another, nor My praise to carved images" (Isaiah 42:8). God does not give His glory to any other god. Yet John wrote that we beheld God's glory in the only begotten Son of God (John 1:14) and that Jesus manifested God's glory (John 2:11). Jesus prayed, "O Father, glorify Me together with Yourself, with the glory which I had with You before the world was" (John 17:5). Jesus is the mighty God.

When Jesus was resurrected from the dead and appeared to the disciples, Thomas was not there. He would not believe the disciples when they told him that Jesus was resurrected unless he saw Jesus' nail-scarred hands and pierced side. When Thomas finally saw the resurrected Christ he exclaimed, "My Lord and my God!" (John 20:28). No one can call anyone this, unless the One he is calling is marked with this honor, for there is only one supreme God.

Even before there was a man who needed to be redeemed, God planned the Incarnation so He could become humanity's Redeemer. Before the world was made, God knew man would sin and that a sinless Lamb would need to be slain to atone for those sins (Revelation 13:8). God formed Adam in His own image (Genesis 1:27). Adam was a "pattern" or "type" of Jesus, the One to come (Romans 5:14). Therefore, with Jesus Christ in mind, God spoke the world into existence. Jesus was God manifested in flesh. Jesus did not come for His own pleasure or to fulfill His human will. His sole purpose was to reconcile fallen humanity back to God. He was the Word of life. "That which was from the beginning, which we have heard, which we have seen with our eyes, which we have looked upon, and our hands have handled, concerning the Word of life" (I John 1:1).

Isaiah said that the Son would be "the Everlasting Father." *Everlasting* means "eternal, forever." *Father* means "chief, God."[19] God is powerful, awesome, and higher than my understanding. Thinking about Him inspires godly fear because I am so small and God is so big. He goes beyond my imagination. When I think of creation—the Grand Canyon, the Himalayan and Andean mountain ranges, the vast oceans and seas—I am overwhelmed by God's greatness.

Besides His creation, there are His mighty acts, such as the exodus of the Israelites from Egypt. They panicked when they came to the western shore of the Red Sea. Mountains blocked any escape to the north or south, and Pharaoh's army bore down on them from the west. God created a diversion; He used the pillar of cloud that guided the Israelites to create a pea-soup fog for the Egyptians. All that night a strong east wind blew across the Red Sea, dividing the waters so the Israelites could cross on the dry seabed. When they had crossed safely to the other side, God lifted the fog off the Egyptians, who charged through the seabed, only to be caught in the collision as the divided waters crashed back together (Exodus 14:20-31). Another awesome demonstration of God's power took place when Elijah confronted the 450 prophets of Baal. Elijah declared, "The God who answers by fire, He is God" (I Kings 18:24). The fire of the Lord blazed down from heaven and consumed the burnt sacrifice, the wood, the stones, and the dust, and even licked up the water in the trench around the altar. Powerful! His awesomeness, power, and authority inspire godly fear in His friends and terror in His enemies.

Yet one day when I was praying and meditating about the everlasting Father, I began to think of Him in a different way. I thought of our own fathers, who lead, guide, protect, provide, discipline, and love compassionately. When I think of God this way, the fear leaves, love fills my heart, and tenderness consumes me. In the same way that I become overwhelmed and speechless in the mightiness of God, I become overwhelmed and speechless in the love of God.

In His mighty acts of creation, the Lord spoke into existence light, the heavens, the earth, the vegetation, and the animals. But when He created man, He took a different approach. As a potter forms a clay vessel, God formed Adam from the dust of the earth and breathed into him the breath of life. When God shaped mankind in His own image and breathed into him the breath of life, it distinguished mankind from all other creation. Man could reason, remember, reflect, make cognitive associations, and communicate. Man had not only a body and spirit, but also an eternal soul. "So God created man in His own image . . . male and female

He created them. Then God blessed them" (Genesis 1:27-28). Here God showed a fatherly attribute of love and blessing. "But now, O LORD, You are our Father; we are the clay, and You our potter; and all we are the work of Your hand" (Isaiah 64:8). Our Father created us in His likeness and He blessed us.

God walked in the Garden of Eden in the cool of the day (Genesis 3:8). He spent time with Adam and Eve, and they were able to communicate with Him. God personally formed them, and He personally maintained a relationship with them; therefore, God became personal to them. He also has a relationship with us. He walks with us, talks with us, cares for us, provides for us, and disciplines us.

When Adam and Eve sinned in the Garden of Eden, God was not pleased with their disobedience. He punished them by making them leave the garden. However, He did not stop communicating with them. He gave them a promise of redemption (Genesis 3:15).

Throughout the Old Testament God talked with, protected, provided for, and disciplined His people. He was a personal God and guide, One they could count on and whose word they could trust. As their Father, He never broke His promises, whether the consequences were blessings or discipline. One of the promises He gave Israel was that He would be their Savior, and this promise applied not only to them but also to all the nations of the earth. "I will say to the north, 'Give them up!' And to the south, 'Do not keep them back!' Bring My sons from afar, and My daughters from the ends of the earth—everyone who is called by My name, whom I have created for My glory; I have formed him, yes, I have made him" (Isaiah 43:6-7). Our Father made this world and formed us for His glory. Whoever carries the name of the Father belongs to Him. "Doubtless You are our Father, though Abraham was ignorant of us, and Israel does not acknowledge us. You, O LORD, are our Father; our Redeemer from Everlasting is Your name" (Isaiah 63:16).

We take on our Father's name through the salvation He has provided. The salvation that was given to the Jews was also given to the Gentiles. We all have the same Father and Redeemer. "Behold, God is my salvation, I will trust and not be afraid; for YAH, the LORD, is my strength and my song; He also has become my salvation" (Isaiah 12:2). Our Father provided salvation for us. He created us for this occasion and for His glory. Our Father is our Redeemer, our Savior, and there is none other (Isaiah 43:11; Hosea 13:4).

In the New Testament, *Father* means "parent."[20] Our everlasting Father is eternal. He has always been. He created everything for His purpose and glory. God is the One responsible for creating the sacrificial Lamb slain for the sins of the world. He is the Father of the "Holy One," the flesh and blood that was conceived in the virgin Mary (Luke 1:35). "He saw that there was no man, and wondered that there was no intercessor; therefore His own arm brought salvation for Him; and His own righteousness, it sustained him" (Isaiah 59:16). God provided His own intercessor because there was no one else on earth who could have done it. Everyone else on earth was tainted by sin.

The Father gave His only begotten Son so that we could be saved through Him. "For there is born to you this day in the city of David a Savior, who is Christ the Lord" (Luke 2:11). There is only one Savior, and that is God. God was manifested in the flesh; He wrought salvation in the form of man. God is a Spirit, and that Spirit became flesh. When John the Baptist saw Jesus he said, "Behold! The Lamb of God who takes away the sin of the world!" (John 1:29).

Jesus was the everlasting Father. Yes, His flesh was mortal, but the Father, the eternal Spirit who dwelled in Jesus, was immortal. He was the Creator who spoke the world into existence.

He overshadowed Mary and created the human image of God. This flesh had a beginning and a purpose. "When the fullness of the time had come, God sent forth His Son, born of a woman, born under the law, to redeem those who were under the law, that we might receive the adoption as sons" (Galatians 4:4-5). Jesus' death on the cross freed those who believe on Him from the curse of the law and slavery to sin, which cleared the way for Him to adopt all believers as His children. We are no longer slaves to sin nor children under the guardianship of the law.[21] All the Old Testament promises concerning this Son came to pass. When the time came, it was done exactly as the everlasting Father wanted it. The Father became our personal Redeemer and Savior.

As stated in Isaiah 9:6, Jesus was both God and man. As a man, He had a Father because He was conceived in Mary, and as a man He acknowledged God as that Father. He acknowledged Himself as the Son because of His humanity. He had all the human traits that you and I have, but as God He also possessed all of God's attributes. He was the mighty God and the everlasting Father. He told Philip, "Believe Me that I am in the Father and the Father in Me, or else believe Me for the sake of the works themselves" (John 14:11). All of Jesus' miracles—from turning the water into wine to raising Lazarus from the dead to healing the lepers to calming the sea—were done through God's command, power, and authority.

Through salvation, the Father becomes personal to us. We are called by our Father's name. Jesus said that He came in His Father's name. He came in His Father's authority and character. He came with the same qualities and traits as the Father. No other human on earth could claim this about himself. Yet Jesus could because He came to do His Father's work. The Father came in the form of man to be our Savior, and it would be through the flesh that He would do His work. "Blessed be the God and Father of our

repentance to Life

Lord Jesus Christ, who has blessed us with every spiritual blessing in the heavenly places in Christ, just as He chose us in Him before the foundation of the world, that we should be holy and without blame before Him in love, having predestined us to adoption as sons by Jesus Christ to Himself, according to the good pleasure of His will, to the praise of the glory of His grace, by which He made us accepted in the Beloved. In Him we have redemption through His blood, the forgiveness of sins, according to the riches of His grace" (Ephesians 1:3-7).

Jesus said that He would not leave us comfortless, or as orphans. He promised, "I will come to you" (John 14:18). Without God we are like children without a father, each one going his own way. Jesus knew that, and He promised that He would not leave us unprotected and unloved but that He would come to us. He would be our Father.

Jesus comes to us as the Comforter, the Holy Spirit. Jesus as a man cannot be with us, but as the Holy Spirit He can. When we are born again, we take on a new name, the name of our Father. We have been adopted as sons and daughters through salvation. "Nor is there salvation in any other, for there is no other name under heaven given among men by which we must be saved" (Acts 4:12). When we are baptized of the water and of the Spirit, we take on Jesus' name. "But when the time had fully come, God sent his Son, born of a woman, born under law, to redeem those under law, that we might receive the full rights of sons. Because you are sons, God sent the Spirit of his Son into our hearts, the Spirit who calls out, 'Abba, Father' " (Galatians 4:4-6, NIV). We take on the Father's name through the salvation He has provided. In John 17, Jesus prayed to His Father: "Father, the hour has come. Glorify Your Son, that Your Son also may glorify You, as You have given Him authority over all flesh, that He should give eternal life to as many as You have given Him" (John

17:1-2). Jesus (the fleshly manifestation of God's Spirit) glorified His Father (the Spirit of God) in His death on the cross as the Savior, and the Father glorified the Son because it would be through Christ that we would have eternal life. On the Day of Pentecost, Peter entreated his immediate audience—and also all men everywhere—to partake of the salvation God had provided through Jesus Christ. "Then Peter said to them, 'Repent, and let every one of you be baptized in the name of Jesus Christ for the remission of sins; and you shall receive the gift of the Holy Spirit'" (Acts 2:38). When we are born again as the Scripture has said, we truly have the Father and the Son; we have the life of the Spirit and the redemptive work of the Son. (See John 14:19-24; Romans 5:6-11; 6:1-11; 8:1-11.)

Isaiah designated to Jesus the title of Prince of Peace. *Prince* means "a head person, governor, lord, master, and ruler." *Peace* means "to be at peace, rest."[22] "Peace I leave with you; my peace I give you. I do not give to you as the world gives" (John 14:27, NIV). The customary good-bye among the Jews was to say *shalom*, meaning "peace." In this passage, Jesus was about to depart, so He added to this farewell by saying, "My peace." This was no conventional wish; this was Jesus' personal, special grant of peace. Because He would be with His followers as the Comforter, His peace would banish fear and dread because they knew Jesus was in control of all circumstances.[23]

In Jesus is the only place we can find true peace and rest. "Come to Me, all you who labor and are heavy laden, and I will give you rest. Take My yoke upon you and learn from Me, for I am gentle and lowly in heart, and you will find rest for your souls" (Matthew 11:28-29). We can come to Jesus with our cares and burdens, and we can find rest for our souls, knowing that He is in control. How does Jesus give us this peace and rest? Paul said, "For the kingdom of God is not eating and drinking,

repentance to Life

but righteousness and peace and joy in the Holy Spirit" (Romans 14:17). Jesus, through the Holy Spirit, gives us peace and rest, and it is glorious (Isaiah 11:10).

God wants us to celebrate and be made whole in Jesus Christ. God wants us to believe in the name of the only begotten Son of God and to partake of Him through His death, burial, and resurrection, which is the gospel.

chapter five

The Gospel According to the Scriptures

What is the gospel? Jesus wanted the gospel preached to every nation, tribe, and tongue. How did the disciples carry out this commission? Now that the disciples are gone, how do we spread the gospel?

When Jesus predicted the destruction of the Temple, His disciples asked Him many questions: "Tell us, when will these things be? And what will be the sign of Your coming, and of the end of the age?" (Matthew 24:3). Jesus gave them a list of signs in verses 4-14, but we want to focus on verse 14. "And this gospel of the kingdom will be preached in all the world as a witness to all the nations, and then the end will come" (Matthew 23:14).

When recording the same event, Mark wrote, "And the gospel must first be preached to all the nations" (Mark 13:10). The gospel was to be preached to all the nations, and the ones with the initial responsibility were the disciples. Shortly before His ascension, Jesus commissioned His disciples: "Go into all the world and preach the gospel to every creature" (Mark 16:15). Because He possessed all authority in heaven and on earth (Matthew 28:18), Jesus told them to go. He wanted the gospel preached to every nation. The apostles were to make disciples by baptizing their converts and teaching them to observe all things that Jesus had commanded them. (See Matthew 28:18-20.) Therefore, by the authority of Jesus Christ, this gospel was not for the Jews only but also for every nation.

Jesus knew that the apostles would pass away long before His second coming, but He wanted to find faith on the earth when

repentance to Life

He returned. He promised He would empower the apostles for this mission. He inspired them as they taught and wrote about Jesus and His commandments. Through word of mouth, through example (living epistles), and through the written Word, the gospel would then be transmitted from generation to generation. Each generation would carry out the great commission. They would teach the commandments of Christ until His return. We have the Scriptures for apostolic examples so we can know how to obey the commandments of Christ.

The commandments of Christ were to baptize "in the name" and to teach converts to observe all the things Jesus had commanded. Jesus promised that He would be with His disciples to the end of the age. He said in John 14:18 that He would not leave his disciples orphans; He would come as a Comforter. These promises apply to every Christian to the end of the age.

All four of the Gospel writers recounted the great commission. In Mark 16:15-18, shortly before His ascension, Jesus told the disciples to go into the world and preach the gospel to every creature. Those who believed and were baptized would be saved; those who refused to believe would be damned. Signs would accompany the believers as they fulfilled the commission: "In My name they will cast out demons; they will speak with new tongues . . . they will lay hands on the sick, and they will recover" (Mark 16:17-18).

Luke added to our knowledge of the event. First, Jesus opened His disciples' understanding so they could comprehend the Scriptures. "Then He said to them, 'Thus it is written, and thus it was necessary for the Christ to suffer and to rise from the dead the third day, and that repentance and remission of sins should be preached in His name to all nations, beginning at Jerusalem. And you are witnesses of these things. Behold, I send the Promise of My Father upon you; but tarry in the city of Jerusalem until you are endued with power from on high' " (Luke 24:46-49).

The disciples needed divine help to understand what was written: Christ would suffer and die and would rise from the dead the third day. Jesus wanted His disciples to understand that they should preach repentance and remission of sins in His name. Their understanding of the task was vital because they were to preach these things to all nations.

John remembered other things about the event. After Jesus arose from the dead, He appeared to the disciples where they were hiding behind closed doors, fearing for their very lives. They were afraid that the Jews would hunt them down. Jesus said, "Peace be with you." He showed them the scars in His hands and His side. Then He said, "As the Father has sent Me, I also send you" (John 20:21). The disciples were to carry on Christ's work. Jesus breathed on them and said, "Receive the Holy Spirit" (John 20:22). The ministry to which Jesus called the disciples required spiritual power. Jesus taught His disciples and endued them with power because they would be the means of founding the church on the day of Pentecost.[24]

Jesus sent the disciples out to preach the gospel message of salvation, and He would not have sent them without enduing them with spiritual power, the promised Holy Spirit. Jesus told the disciples to go to Jerusalem where they would receive that promise. This promised Holy Spirit would fill the apostolic message with divine power. (See Acts 1:8.) However, the promised Holy Spirit was not just for the disciples; it was for everyone else who received and obeyed the gospel of Christ. (See Acts 2:39.)

The apostles were to preach Christ according to the Scriptures. Jesus suffered and died for the sins of the world; He was

repentance to Life

buried and rose again the third day, according to the Scriptures. Repentance and remission of sins were to be preached in Jesus' name, and baptism was to be administered in His name according to the Scriptures. Jesus would fill them with the Holy Spirit according to the Scriptures.

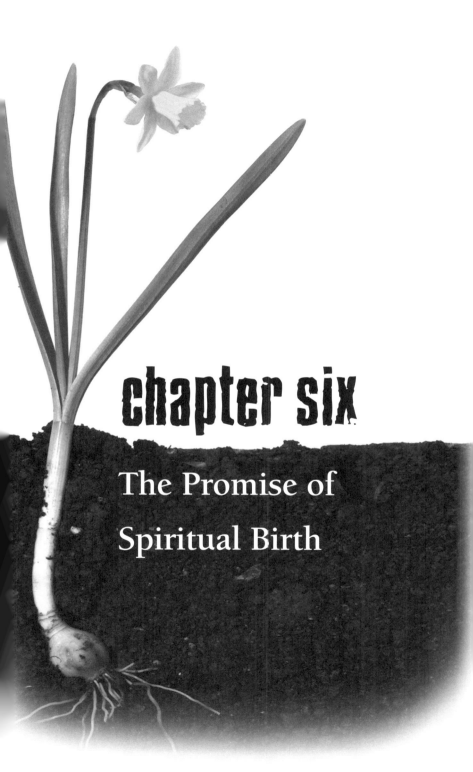

chapter six

The Promise of Spiritual Birth

Jesus was very specific about what one must do to enter the kingdom of God. We find His instructions in all four Gospels. However, John is the only Gospel that records Jesus' meetings with Nicodemus and with the Samaritan woman at the well. Nicodemus, a Pharisee and member of the Sanhedrin, came to Jesus by night. He told Jesus that many believed He was a teacher come from God because no one else could perform miracles as Jesus did unless God was with Him.

Apparently Nicodemus had risked meeting with the rabbi to discuss His origins, but, like the wind, Jesus "blew" the conversation a different way. Jesus said, "Most assuredly, I say to you, unless one is born again, he cannot see the kingdom of God" (John 3:3). Startled, Nicodemus asked, "'How can a man be born when he is old? Can he enter a second time into his mother's womb and be born?' Jesus answered, 'Most assuredly, I say to you, unless one is born of water and the Spirit, he cannot enter the kingdom of God. That which is born of the flesh is flesh, and that which is born of the Spirit is spirit. Do not marvel that I said to you, "You must be born again." The wind blows where it wishes, and you hear the sound of it, but cannot tell where it comes from and where it goes. So is everyone who is born of the Spirit'" (John 3:4-8).

Even though Nicodemus, as a ruler of the Jews, should have been well versed in the Scriptures and Jesus expected him to know about spiritual birth, Nicodemus acted like he had never heard about it. The concept confused him. But this spiritual birth was obviously important since Jesus said without it one could not enter the kingdom of God. Jesus did not reveal to Nicodemus exactly what would happen when a person was born of the Spirit, but He did explain what He meant by being "born again." He said that whatever is born of flesh is flesh, but to partake of spiritual birth one must be born of the Spirit. Jesus compared being born of the Spirit to the wind. The wind blows wherever it wants, and people can hear it, but they do not know where it comes from or where it goes. Likewise, when a person is born of the Spirit he or she will hear the sound of it but will not know where it comes from or where it goes. Jesus said this would happen to everyone who is born of the Spirit.

Shortly after His meeting with Nicodemus, Jesus traveled to Samaria. While His disciples were in the city getting food, Jesus rested by the ancient well that Jacob had dug. While He rested in the heat of the day, a Samaritan woman came to draw water. Jesus asked her for a drink. The woman was nonplussed because social conventions of the day would not have permitted a Jewish man to speak to a Samaritan woman. She asked, "'How is it that You, being a Jew, ask a drink from me, a Samaritan woman?' For Jews have no dealings with Samaritans. Jesus answered and said to her, 'If you knew the gift of God, and who it is who says to you, "Give Me a drink," you would have asked Him, and He would have given you living water.' The woman said to Him, 'Sir, you have nothing to draw with, and the well is deep. Where then do You get that living water? Are You greater than our father Jacob, who gave us the well, and drank from it himself, as well as his sons and his livestock?'" (John 4:9-12).

Here again, Jesus was talking about a subject that this woman did not understand: Living Water. Jesus said, "If you knew the gift of God." What was the gift of God? Living Water! If this woman had

The Promise of Spiritual Birth

known that the gift of God was Living Water, she could have asked Jesus for it, and He would have given her Living Water. But she did not know who Jesus was or what He was talking about. She thought Jesus was going to get this "living water" from an earthly well. Jesus explained, "Whoever drinks of this water will thirst again, but whoever drinks of the water that I shall give him will never thirst. But the water that I shall give him will become in him a fountain of water springing up into everlasting life" (John 4:13-14).

The woman of Samaria would continually come to Jacob's well to draw water because she would continue to get thirsty. However, the Living Water Jesus offers will be in us a continual flowing, and we will never thirst again. The gift of God is Living Water; anyone who drinks of it will live forever.

Another account found only in John concerns the Bread of Life. Jesus explained this extensively, yet the crowd did not understand Him. The day before, the crowd had witnessed the miracle of Jesus feeding the five thousand (John 6:1-14). The next day they found Him on the other side of the sea. They asked, "Rabbi, when did You come here?" (John 6:25). As He often did, instead of answering the question, Jesus cut to the heart of the matter. He told the crowd that they had looked for Him not because of the miracle but because their stomachs had been filled. He told them to look instead for the food that endures to eternal life. They wondered what they should do to work the works of God. Jesus replied, "This is the work of God, that you believe in Him whom He sent" (John 6:29). From this, the people must have understood that Jesus was claiming to be the Messiah because they asked for a sign—despite the fact that they had just seen Him feed five thousand with five barley loaves and two small fish! They wanted to know what work Jesus would do; after all, Moses had given them bread from heaven to eat. Jesus replied, "Moses did not give you the bread from heaven, but My

repentance to Life

Father gives you the true bread from heaven. For the bread of God is He who comes down from heaven and gives life to the world" (John 6:32-33). The crowd was eager for this miraculous bread. Jesus said, "I am the bread of life. He who comes to Me shall never hunger, and he who believes in Me shall never thirst" (John 6:35).

Jesus was the Bread that came down from heaven. Just as He told the Samaritan woman and now the Jews, if they would believe in Christ and come to Him, they would never again hunger or thirst. This was hard for the crowd to understand because they did not perceive Jesus as the Messiah. They said, "Is not this Jesus, the son of Joseph, whose father and mother we know? How is it then that He says, 'I have come down from heaven'?" (John 6:42).

Jesus continued to describe Himself as the Bread of Life: "Most assuredly, I say to you, he who believes in Me has everlasting life. I am the bread of life. Your fathers ate the manna in the wilderness, and are dead. This is the bread which comes down from heaven, that one may eat of it and not die. I am the living bread which came down from heaven. If anyone eats of this bread, he will live forever; and the bread that I shall give is My flesh, which I shall give for the life of the world" (John 6:47-51).

Jesus explained that if they would believe in Him, they would have eternal life. He was the Bread of Life, and if they ate of this bread they would not die. The Jews did not understand, for they said among themselves, "How can this Man give us His flesh to eat?" (John 6:52).

Jesus answered, "Most assuredly, I say to you, unless you eat the flesh of the Son of Man and drink His blood, you have no life in you" (John 6:53). Anyone who does not eat of the flesh of Christ or drink His blood has not been born again but is spiritually dead. Jesus said, "Whoever eats My flesh and drinks My blood has eternal life, and I will raise him up at the last day. For My flesh is food indeed, and My blood is drink indeed. He who eats My flesh and drinks My blood abides in Me, and I in him" (John 6:54-56).

John gave us three metaphors that Jesus used to explain spiritual birth: wind, living water, and life-giving bread, which Jesus enlarged to include both His flesh and His blood. With each metaphor, Jesus persisted with the truth that unless believers partook of the wind, the water, or the bread (all of which stood for Himself) they could not partake of eternal life.

Jesus told Nicodemus that unless he was born again of water and Spirit, he could not enter the kingdom of God. What then was the kingdom of God? Jesus said, "The kingdom of God is within you" (Luke 17:21). It was not an earthly kingdom like Palestine or Syria. Matthew, Mark, and Luke all recounted Jesus' declaration that some under the sound of His voice would not see death until they had "seen" the kingdom of God coming with power (Matthew 16:28; Mark 9:1; Luke 9:27). The kingdom of God was not a tangible kingdom people could see physically, but it was an inward kingdom. So what was the kingdom of God? It was the promised Holy Spirit!

When Jesus talked to Nicodemus about the wind, the Samaritan woman about the living water, and the unbelieving crowd about the bread of life, He was referring to the promise of the Holy Spirit. On the last day of the Feast of Tabernacles, Jesus cried out, "'If anyone thirsts, let him come to Me and drink. He who believes in Me, as the Scripture has said, out of his heart will flow rivers of living water.' But this He spoke concerning the Spirit, whom those believing in Him would receive; for the Holy Spirit was not yet given, because Jesus was not yet glorified" (John 7:37-39). So the wind and the water and the bread were the promised Holy Spirit!

Jesus used metaphors of wind, living water, and bread of life to describe spiritual birth. These were not different gospels. There was only one way to partake of spiritual birth, for these all had the same meaning. This promised spiritual birth would happen to believers after Jesus ascended into heaven.

The promised Holy Spirit was not given, because Jesus was still with them. Jesus told the disciples, "It is to your advantage that I go away; for if I do not go away, the Helper will not come to you; but if I depart, I will send Him to you" (John 16:7). John the Baptist prophesied of the One who would baptize with the Holy Spirit. The Spirit had told him how to recognize Him: "Upon whom you see the Spirit descending, and remaining on Him, this is He who baptizes with the Holy Spirit" (John 1:33). Jesus is the One who baptizes with the Holy Spirit.

Jesus told the disciples to go to Jerusalem to wait for the promise of the Father, which was the Holy Spirit. The disciples would be the first to experience it, and, for the first time, they would preach repentance and remission of sins in His name; they would baptize in His name, and they would teach men the commandments of Christ. Then the apostles would preach the gospel and fulfill Christ's commission.

chapter seven

The Promised Holy Spirit

The Promised Holy Spirit

john the baptist prophesied, "He will baptize you with the Holy Spirit and fire" (Matthew 3:11). Jesus said, "But the Helper, the Holy Spirit, whom the Father will send in My name. . ." (John 14:26). Jesus said, "Behold, I send the Promise of My Father upon you; but tarry in the city of Jerusalem until you are endued with power from on high" (Luke 24:49). Jesus said, "There are some standing here who will not taste death till they see the kingdom of God present with power" (Mark 9:1).

John the Baptist prophesied about One who would baptize with the Holy Spirit and with fire. That One was Jesus. Jesus said that the Father would send the Holy Spirit in His name. He told the disciples to wait in Jerusalem for the promised Holy Spirit. Jesus assured them that there were some standing before Him who would not see death until they saw the Holy Spirit come with power. All of these New Testament promises of the coming of the Holy Spirit had already been prophesied in the Old Testament. "Until the Spirit is poured upon us from on high" (Isaiah 32:15). (See Joel 2:28; Zechariah 12:10; 14:8; Ezekiel 36:27.)

The promised Holy Spirit had never yet been given in this manner. It could not be until Jesus accomplished what He had come to do. (See Isaiah 53.) The Holy Spirit was not given until Jesus was glorified (John 7:37-39). "Exalted to the right hand of God, he has received from the Father the promised Holy Spirit and has poured out what you now see and hear" (Acts 2:33, NIV).

repentance to Life

This promise, Jesus said, was for anyone who hungered and thirsted after righteousness (Matthew 5:6). (See John 4:14; 6:35; 7:37.) While this promise was for whosoever will, it was also a command. (See Joel 2:32; Matthew 28:20; Acts 2:21, 39; 10:33, 42, 48; 17:30; Romans 16:26.)

In Acts 1:2 Luke referred to the commandments Jesus had given to the apostles. These commandments were as follows:
1. To make disciples of all nations;
2. To baptize them in the name of the Father, Son, and the Holy Spirit;
3. To teach them to observe all things that Jesus had commanded the disciples;
4. To preach the gospel to everyone: repentance and remission of sins.

The Holy Spirit would be poured out first in Jerusalem, and the apostles would witness it. They would receive the promised Living Water. Zechariah wrote, "In that day it shall be that living waters shall flow from Jerusalem" (Zechariah 14:8).

The Book of Acts is a continuation of Luke's Gospel. In Acts we see the promise of the Holy Spirit fulfilled. Luke wrote, "And being assembled together with them [the apostles], [Jesus] commanded them not to depart from Jerusalem, but to wait for the Promise of the Father, 'which,' He said, 'you have heard from Me'" (Acts 1:4). (See Luke 24:49.) Jesus continued, "For John truly baptized with water, but you shall be baptized with the Holy Spirit not many days from now" (Acts 1:5). The promised Holy Spirit was coming, and Jesus told them to wait in Jerusalem because that was where the Spirit would be poured out. The prophecy was about to be fulfilled, and He did not want them to miss it. Jesus had spent a lot of time with these men and others, and they were about to experience the greatest gift, which the Old Testament prophets wrote about but were not able to experience. (See I Peter 1:10-12.)

This promise would start with the Jews but would spread to the Samaritans and from there across the then known world. "You shall receive power when the Holy Spirit has come upon you; and you shall be witnesses to Me in Jerusalem, and in all Judea and Samaria, and to the end of the earth" (Acts 1:8). Jesus told the apostles that they would be preaching this gospel to people of other nations. This baptism of the Holy Spirit would give them power to preach the gospel as Jesus had commissioned them. They would see the kingdom of God come with power. Future generations also would see this same Spirit come with power, and we, too, are commissioned to preach this same gospel.

chapter eight

The Promise Has Come

The Promise Has Come

all the verses of Scripture we have used so far concerning the promised Holy Spirit were fulfilled at Pentecost. Those same verses of Scriptures will carry on through the years and apply to anyone who hungers and thirsts and comes to Jesus to be filled.

"When the Day of Pentecost had fully come, they were all with one accord in one place. And suddenly there came a sound from heaven, as of a rushing mighty wind, and it filled the whole house where they were sitting. Then there appeared to them divided tongues, as of fire, and one sat upon each of them. And they were all filled with the Holy Spirit and began to speak with other tongues, as the Spirit gave them utterance" (Acts 2:1-4). Besides the eleven disciples, there were over 100 people who waited in Jerusalem, praying for the promised Holy Spirit. They were not complaining about what Jesus had told them to do or just talking about everyday things; they were praying and they were in agreement. Their sole purpose was to receive the baptism of the Holy Spirit that Jesus said He would send.

When the appointed time came, they heard what sounded like a hurricane-force wind from heaven. Divided tongues as of fire rested on each of them, and they were all filled with the Holy Spirit. They were all filled because they were all there for the same reason. They all began to speak with other tongues as the Spirit gave them utterance; these languages were unknown to the speakers. They were being reborn from above as Jesus breathed into them the breath of life.

repentance to Life

Jesus had explained this phenomenon to Nicodemus when He told the baffled Jewish ruler about spiritual birth being likened to the wind: "The wind blows wherever it pleases. You hear its sound, but you cannot tell where it comes from or where it is going. So it is with everyone born of the Spirit" (John 3:8, NIV). The Spirit is like the wind: you cannot see the Spirit, and you cannot tell where it comes from or where it is going, but you can hear it. What happened to the 120 in the upper room happens to everyone who is born of the Spirit.

The 120 were all in one place, praying and worshiping God. Jesus had told the woman at the well, "Yet a time is coming and has now come when the true worshipers will worship the Father in spirit and in truth, for they are the kind of worshipers the Father seeks. God is spirit, and his worshipers must worship in spirit and in truth" (John 4:23-24, NIV). These upper room promise-seekers were filled with the Holy Spirit as they worshiped God in spirit and in truth. When the Spirit came into their lives, they could not see Him, but they could hear the sound, for they all spoke with tongues as the Spirit gave them utterance. This happens to everyone who is born of the Spirit.[25]

This was the Holy Spirit Jesus had promised. John the Baptist had told everyone that One was coming who would be the Holy Spirit baptizer. This baptism of the Spirit was not just for the apostles, the 120 in the upper room, and the three thousand who received it after Peter's sermon. No, it did not stop there; it would be a continual outpouring on whomever hungered and thirsted for it and who worshiped in spirit and in truth. The promise was not exclusive but inclusive. The issue was not the color of people's skin, their country of origin, their possession of money and lands, or the location of their worship place. The issue was not *where* they worshiped or *who* they were; the issue was *how* and *whom* they worshiped.

This baptism of the Holy Spirit is the Living Water Jesus told the Samaritan woman about. This is the Comforter Jesus said He would send. This is the long-awaited fulfillment of the Old Testament prophecies. This is Christ in you, the hope of glory!

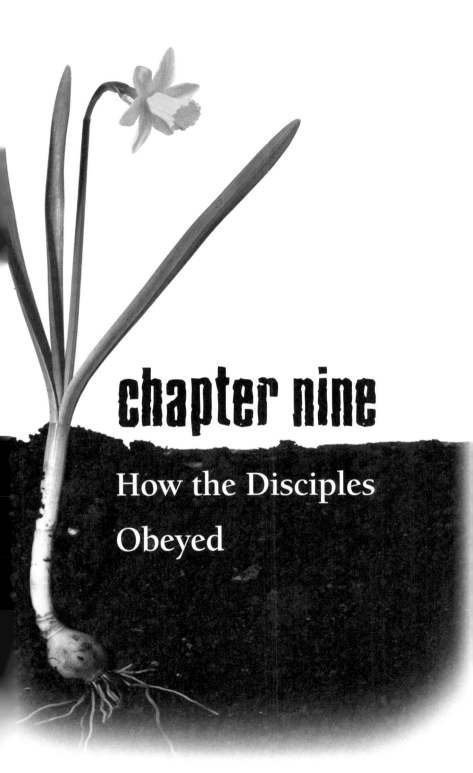

chapter nine

How the Disciples Obeyed

"**but you shall** receive power when the Holy Spirit has come upon you; and you shall be witnesses to Me in Jerusalem, and in all Judea and Samaria, and to the end of the earth" (Acts 1:8). Jesus promised to give the disciples power to preach the gospel. They were to start in Jerusalem and Judea, then branch out to Samaria and beyond. Jesus told the disciples, "All authority in heaven and on earth has been given to me. Therefore go and make disciples of all nations, baptizing them in the name of the Father and of the Son and of the Holy Spirit, and teaching them to obey everything I have commanded you. And surely I am with you always, to the very end of the age" (Matthew 28:18-20, NIV).

Now that the disciples had received the Holy Spirit and the power that came with it, they could begin working on what Jesus had commissioned them to do. They had to obey and present the gospel in the way Jesus had commanded them: to make disciples and equip them to help preach this gospel to the whole world. Every disciple was under Jesus' command to obey the gospel in the same way He had taught the apostles.

The promised Holy Spirit came first to the 120 who had assembled in the upper room in a house in Jerusalem. This was during the Feast of Pentecost, and Jews from many nations had gathered to celebrate the feast. The roaring of the wind and the commotion of 120 people worshiping and speaking in tongues drew a huge crowd. Many curiosity seekers were astonished when they saw and heard the worshipers, who had spilled out into the street—whom they recognized as Galileans—speaking in their various native languages. Galileans were known as common folk who would not be trained in other languages. They spoke Aramaic and perhaps Greek, the universal language of the Greco-Roman world, but to speak in this many different languages would be beyond their linguistic capabilities.[26] The crowd was perplexed because there was no suitable explanation for this phenomenon. They heard simple Galileans speaking in many languages of the "mighty deeds and the magnitude of God."[27] The crowd knew this was something not normally within the comprehension of common folk. Many were awed, but some reacted with loud mockery and contempt. Seeing the overjoyed antics of the worshipers, they thought the worshipers must be drunk.

Jesus had given Peter the keys to the kingdom (Matthew 16:18-19) and with these keys the authority to "unlock" the door of salvation to the Jews first at Jerusalem. Peter, who had committed an act of cowardice when he denied any affiliation with Jesus, now, filled with the power of the Spirit, boldly stood before an astonished, awed, and mocking crowd of more than three thousand. The other apostles stood with Peter in a show of solidarity and agreement. This action arrested the attention of the crowd, but Peter still had to raise his voice to be heard.

Peter had not prepared or memorized a sermon, but he had Christ in him. "Men of Judea and all who dwell in Jerusalem, let this be known to you, and heed my words. For these are not drunk, as you suppose" (Acts 2:14-15). Many of these Jews feared God and believed the Scriptures; Peter wanted to open their understanding to the fact that this outpouring of the Holy Spirit was a fulfillment of Scripture. "This is what was spoken by the prophet Joel: *'And it shall come to pass in the last days, says God, that I will pour out of My Spirit on all flesh'*" (Acts 2:16-17). Peter quoted from

Joel 2:28-32. He said that what the worshipers had received from above was what Joel had prophesied would happen. The Spirit had been poured out and was available to all people.

This Jewish crowd needed to hear Peter's message before faith could awaken in their hearts, enabling them to call on their Savior for salvation. Because he had the keys to the kingdom, Peter was the one who preached Christ to them on this initiation day. Peter explained what Jesus had just given to the 120: "Exalted to the right hand of God [signifying authority and not a physical position], he has received from the Father the promised Holy Spirit and has poured out what you now see and hear" (Acts 2:33, NIV). What they saw and heard were expressions of joy and the 120 speaking with tongues as the Spirit gave them utterance. Peter cited Psalm 110:1, a psalm that the Jews knew referred to the Messiah: *"The LORD said to my Lord, 'Sit at My right hand, till I make Your enemies Your footstool'"* (Acts 2:34-35). Peter then applied this verse to Jesus Christ, the One who had taught them, given His life to atone for the sins of the world, risen again, taught His disciples for forty days, and then ascended. Peter concluded, "Therefore let all the house of Israel know assuredly that God has made this Jesus, whom you crucified, both Lord and Christ" (Acts 2:36).

This declaration that Jesus was both Lord (whom the Jews knew as Jehovah) and Christ (their long-awaited Messiah) suddenly opened the Jews' eyes to the heinous crime they had committed. Their hearts were convicted; what could they do to obtain forgiveness for this sin? Peter's reply was in perfect accordance with the commission Jesus had given: "Repent, and let every one of you be baptized in the name of Jesus Christ for the remission of sins; and you shall receive the gift of the Holy Spirit" (Acts 2:38). Peter obeyed the commission of Jesus Christ; Jesus had told the apostles to teach their converts to observe all the things He had commanded them.

repentance to Life

Repentance and water baptism go together. The idea of an unbaptized Christian was completely foreign to the New Testament.[28] Baptism was not a new concept for the Jews. For centuries, they had baptized their proselytized converts in a ritual bath, or *mikveh*. This ceremony cleansed away the convert's former life.[29] When John the Baptist came and preached repentance and remission of sins, he baptized his converts in preparation for the coming Messiah (Mark 1:4). Now Peter preached baptism for the remission of sins, and, in obedience to Christ's commission, it had to be administered in Jesus' name. When we repent, are baptized, and receive the Holy Spirit, we are identifying with Jesus' death, burial, and resurrection. The gospel Peter preached was just that: repentance and baptism in Jesus' name for the remission of sins. Peter said, "You shall receive the gift of the Holy Spirit" (Acts 2:38).

Peter knew of only one baptism of the Holy Spirit, and that was the one he had just received. Jesus had told Nicodemus about this spiritual birth (John 3:5), and Peter preached it on the Day of Pentecost. Jesus had said of Himself, "I am the door. If anyone enters by Me, he will be saved" (John 10:9). As Peter preached, he used the keys to the kingdom to "unlock" the door of salvation.

If you want to enter the door of salvation, it must be through Jesus. You will draw water from the well of salvation by obeying what Peter said in Acts 2:38. This salvation has been promised to you, for Peter said, "The promise is to you and to your children, and to all who are afar off, as many as the Lord our God will call" (Acts 2:39).

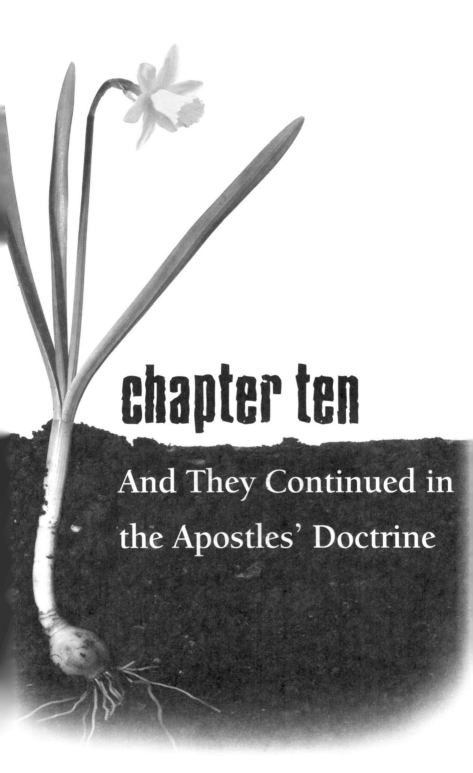

chapter ten

And They Continued in the Apostles' Doctrine

"Then Peter said to them, 'Repent, and let every one of you be baptized in the name of Jesus Christ for the remission of sins; and you shall receive the gift of the Holy Spirit'" (Acts 2:38). As Peter preached on the Day of Pentecost, the eleven apostles stood with him; they were in unified agreement about the first apostolic message preached. What Peter said that day was what Jesus had commissioned the apostles to do before He ascended into heaven.

Peter's powerful sermon was longer than what is recorded in Acts 2. We do not know exactly what else he said, but we do know that Peter pleaded with the crowd to be saved "from this corrupt generation" (Acts 2:40, NIV).

When we are preaching the gospel, we can read Peter's words to the generation we live in. The warning and the pleading are just as important now as they were then. Not everyone received Peter's words that day, and not everyone will receive ours. The ones who did receive his words were baptized. "Then those who gladly received his word were baptized; and that day about three thousand souls were added to them" (Acts 2:41). Even though Luke did not write that they received the Holy Spirit, that does not mean that they did not receive it. When he wrote that they "were baptized," we can undoubtedly assume that it means they were baptized in Jesus' name, since that is what Peter had just commanded.

repentance to Life

Can we take this verse of Scripture that says, "they were baptized" to mean they were baptized with both water and Spirit? Peter's command was very clear, and what he told them in verse 38 had not changed by verse 41. Luke did not have to spell it out for us to know how it was done. When Peter instructed them concerning what they needed to do to be saved, they did it. Three thousand souls were added to the new community of believers because they obeyed Peter's words.

"And they continued steadfastly in the apostles' doctrine and fellowship, in the breaking of bread, and in prayers" (Acts 2:42). *Steadfastly* means they continued "earnestly towards, to be constantly diligent, to adhere closely to, unwavering"[30] in the apostles' doctrine, which followed the commands of Jesus.

I am sure a lot of things were said in chapter 2 that were not recorded, but everything that was recorded is important for us to know. From the inception of the Christian church the apostles taught and observed exactly what Jesus had instructed them to do in His name.

In Acts 3, Peter and John were on their way to the Temple to pray when they came upon a lame man begging for money. Peter and John had no money to give, but Peter gave him a far greater gift. Peter said to the lame man, "In the name of Jesus Christ of Nazareth, rise up and walk" (Acts 3:6). Instantly, the lame man began to leap and walk and praise God in the Temple. The people who saw the man knew that he had been lame and they were filled with wonder and amazement, looking at Peter and John as if they had some mystical powers. Peter assured the onlookers that the miracle had happened through believing in the power of Jesus' name. Since a crowd had gathered, Peter preached a message like the one he had preached on the Day of Pentecost.

"And His name, through faith in His name, has made this man strong, whom you see and know. Yes, the faith which comes through Him has given him this perfect soundness in the presence of you all" (Acts 3:16). It is through faith in Jesus that healing is accomplished, and only through the name of Jesus Christ are these promises fulfilled. Mark recorded that Jesus, as He commissioned the apostles, told them what signs would follow those who believed in Him. "And these signs will follow those who believe: In My name they will cast out demons; they will speak with new tongues; they will take up serpents; and if they drink anything deadly, it will by no means hurt them; they will lay hands on the sick, and they will recover" (Mark 16:17-18).

Just as he had told the crowd on the Day of Pentecost, Peter told these Jews to repent. They had to turn from their wicked ways and turn to God so that their sins could be blotted out (Acts 3:19). His message had not changed; it was still repentance, water baptism in Jesus' name for the remission of sins, and the infilling of the Holy Spirit. This was being born of the water and the Spirit.

Later, Paul wrote, "When the kindness and love of God our Savior appeared, he saved us, not because of righteous things we had done, but because of his mercy. He saved us through the washing of rebirth and renewal by the Holy Spirit, whom he poured out on us generously through Jesus Christ our Savior" (Titus 3:4-6, NIV). We were saved not by our righteousness—for our righteousness is but filthy rags—but by the mercy of God. He saved us through the washing (baptism) of rebirth and revived us by the Holy Spirit. "Do you not know that as many of us as were baptized into Christ Jesus were baptized into His death? Therefore we were buried with Him through baptism into death, that just as Christ was raised from the dead by the glory of the Father, even so we also should walk in newness of life" (Romans 6:3-4).

In Acts 4, Peter and John were arrested for preaching in Jesus' name and for healing the lame man. Peter told the Sanhedrin, the Jewish council, that they were responsible for Jesus' crucifixion

repentance to Life

but He had risen from the dead. It was because of Jesus that the lame man stood before them healed. The Sanhedrin could not deny this notable miracle, so they released Peter and John with instructions not to speak or teach in the name of Jesus. They wanted to stop the spreading of the apostles' doctrine because they were afraid it would overtake the city.

Of course, the apostles did not obey the Sanhedrin. In Acts 5 they were again thrown in prison for teaching and for healing the sick. But an angel of the Lord came at night and set them free. The angel told them to stand in the Temple and preach to the people. When the officers came to the prison to get Peter and John, they were astonished because the two preachers were gone. The council was confounded until a messenger came to tell them, "Look, the men whom you put in prison are standing in the temple and teaching the people!" (Acts 5:25). The officers went to the Temple, arrested the apostles, and brought them back to face the council. "Did we not strictly command you not to teach in this name? And look, you have filled Jerusalem with your doctrine, and intend to bring this Man's blood on us!" (Acts 5:28). Peter and the other apostles answered the charge: "We ought to obey God rather than men. The God of our fathers raised up Jesus whom you murdered by hanging on a tree. Him God has exalted to His right hand to be Prince and Savior, to give repentance to Israel and forgiveness of sins. And we are His witnesses to these things, and so also is the Holy Spirit whom God has given to those who obey Him" (Acts 5:29-32).

Here again are the familiar themes of apostolic preaching: Jesus had risen and ascended. He now gave the Holy Spirit to those who repented and obeyed the gospel. The apostles and the Holy Spirit were witnesses of these things because the apostles and the other believers had received Him. All who were obedient to the apostles' doctrine repented, were baptized in Jesus' name, and received the Holy Spirit.

Therefore, after Pentecost the apostles continued to preach the same message, although not everyone accepted it. Paul later wrote, "They have not all obeyed the gospel. For Isaiah says, *'Lord, who has believed our report?'* So then faith comes by hearing, and hearing by the word of God" (Romans 10:16-17). Some people allow the gospel to change their lives, while others reject it. Those who believe and obey the gospel have for their foundation the apostles and prophets with Jesus Christ as the chief cornerstone (Ephesians 2:20).

chapter eleven

The Samaritans Received the Living Water

"but you shall receive power when the Holy Spirit has come upon you; and you shall be witnesses to Me in Jerusalem, and in all Judea and Samaria, and to the end of the earth" (Acts 1:8). This chapter recounts the spread of the gospel from the Jews to the Samaritans. Earlier in this study, we saw that Jesus, when He talked with the woman at the well, had planted a seed of the promise that was to come to the Samaritans. Jesus told the woman, "If you knew the gift of God and who it is that asks you for a drink, you would have asked him and he would have given you living water" (John 4:10, NIV).

The living water was the Holy Spirit. It had been poured out on the Jews first and now it was to be poured out on the Samaritans. The Samaritans were a mixed race. When Sargon of Assyria destroyed Samaria in 721 BC, he deported thousands of Jews and sent in people of other lands he had conquered to resettle the area, resulting in intermarriage between the races. After this, the Jews traditionally despised the Samaritans and did not associate with them (John 4:9). However, Joel had prophesied that God would pour out His Spirit on *all* flesh (Joel 2:28). Paul wrote, "You are all sons of God through faith in Christ Jesus. For as many of you as were baptized into Christ have put on Christ. There is neither Jew nor Greek, there is neither slave nor free, there is neither male nor female; for you are all one in Christ Jesus. And if you are Christ's, then you are Abraham's seed, and heirs according to the promise" (Galatians 3:26-29). When we are born of the water and the Spirit we are baptized into Christ Jesus, and we are Abraham's seed and heirs according to the promise no matter what our race or ethnicity.

The church in Jerusalem had grown into the thousands. The Jewish leaders were increasingly nervous about the possibility of the Jesus movement taking over the city. They recruited young and zealous Saul of Tarsus, a student of Gamaliel, and told him to destroy this "seditious sect." Stephen's death may have acted as a trigger for increased persecution. Saul declared an all-out war, and many Bible scholars think that the Greek language describing this event denoted that Saul was like a wild boar on a rampage.[31] He put followers of the Way in prison and cast his vote for the death of some (Acts 26:10). (These actions would later cause Saul, who became Paul, to suffer deep remorse. See Galatians 1:13 and I Timothy 1:13.)

To escape Saul's onslaught, many Jerusalem saints scattered across the countryside, preaching the gospel everywhere they went. One of these was Philip, one of the seven leaders chosen in Acts 6:5. Full of the Holy Spirit, Philip fled to Samaria, where he preached the word. "Multitudes with one accord heeded the things spoken by Philip" and were baptized in the name of the Lord Jesus, and many were healed and delivered of demonic spirits (Acts 8:6-7, 16). Joy filled the city!

Their spiritual birth was not complete, though, because none of the Samaritans who had believed, repented, and been baptized in Jesus' name had yet received the Holy Spirit. Peter and John journeyed to Samaria, laid their hands on these believers, and prayed for them. Their demonstrations of joy when they received the Holy Spirit must have been phenomenal because a sorcerer named Simon offered to buy the ability to perform this amazing "trick." Therefore, even though the Bible does not say that the baptized Samaritans spoke with tongues when they received the Holy Spirit, they had to have been doing something more than standing quietly accepting the Lord Jesus Christ as their personal Savior, a "trick" Simon the sorcerer would never have wanted to buy. The Samaritans had received the Living Water Jesus had promised them in John 4. Their spiritual birth was now complete.

We learn from this event that the Holy Spirit is not an optional, added blessing that is available to believers but that is not necessary for salvation. Receiving the Holy Spirit is just as essential to spiritual birth as it was for the Spirit of God to breathe the breath of life into Adam. We are spiritually dead until the Holy Spirit has breathed the breath of eternal life into us. Philip's revival among the Samaritans was accompanied by many signs, but one of the essential signs—speaking with tongues as evidence of the indwelling Holy Spirit—was missing until Peter and John came and laid their hands on them and prayed for them.

If the worshiping, praise, and joy of the Samaritans had been enough, Philip would not have needed Peter. Philip knew the apostolic salvation message. He knew the Samaritans needed to believe on the One about whom he was preaching. After they believed and repented, Philip baptized them in Jesus' name. But Philip knew the Samaritans had not yet received the Holy Spirit because he had not heard the "sound" that is the sign of everyone who is born of the Spirit; none of them had spoken with tongues. After Peter and John prayed for them, everyone knew that the Samaritans had received the Holy Spirit because they heard the "sound" of the Spirit.

After Philip's successful revival in Samaria, the Lord told him to go southward until he found the road that connected Jerusalem with Gaza. The Lord did not tell Philip why he must travel more than forty miles, but when he found the road, Philip spotted an obviously wealthy man being "chauffeured" in a well-appointed chariot, no doubt part of a caravan. The Lord told Philip to catch

repentance to Life

up to the chariot. As he neared, Philip heard the chariot passenger reading from a Hebrew scroll of Isaiah. Arresting the man's attention, Philip asked, "Do you understand what you are reading?" (Acts 8:30). The man replied, "How can I, unless someone guides me?" (Acts 8:31), and he invited Philip to join him in the chariot.

Philip learned that the man was Ethiopia's minister of finance, serving under Queen Candace.[32] He was returning from a pilgrimage to Jerusalem (Acts 8:28). Many first-century Gentiles had grown weary of the pantheon of pagan gods and the gross immorality that was part of their rites of worship. Many of these Gentiles began to search in Judaism for truth and became proselytes to the Jewish faith. Those who did not become proselytes but who attended Jewish synagogues were called "God-fearers."[33] It is uncertain into which category this Ethiopian fit, but he was obviously desiring to know more about the one true God as he searched through Isaiah.

Philip looked at the place on the scroll where the Ethiopian's finger pointed: "He was led as a sheep to the slaughter; and as a lamb before its shearer is silent, so He opened not His mouth. In His humiliation His justice was taken away, and who will declare His generation? For His life is taken from the earth" (Acts 8:32-33).

The Ethiopian asked, "Of whom does the prophet say this, of himself or of some other man?" (Acts 8:34). Philip immediately recognized this as a passage from Isaiah 53 that described the Messiah's suffering and death. What a perfect opportunity to preach the gospel of Jesus to this Ethiopian! Philip obviously taught him the apostles' doctrine, because when they came to an oasis the Ethiopian exclaimed, "See, here is water. What hinders me from being baptized?"

Philip replied, "If you believe with all your heart, you may."

The Ethiopian declared, "I believe that Jesus Christ is the Son of God" (Acts 8:36-37). The Ethiopian ordered the chariot stopped, and Philip accompanied him into the water and baptized him. (We know that Philip immersed the Ethiopian because Acts 8:38-39 said, "[they] went down into the water. . . . they came up out of the water.")

Philip's entire lesson was not recorded here. But we know that Philip preached Jesus to the Samaritans, and he would not have preached a different gospel to the Ethiopian. Paul later wrote, "There is one body and one Spirit, just as you were called in one hope of your calling; one Lord, one faith, one baptism; one God and Father of all, who is above all, and through all, and in you all" (Ephesians 4:4-6). We have seen that Philip preached repentance, baptism in Jesus' name, and receiving the Holy Spirit to the Samaritans. Philip was under the mandate of Christ's commands; therefore, he adhered to, obeyed, and preached the apostles' doctrine.

We do not have the right to change the gospel to fit our opinions or desires. We could no more change the process of spiritual birth than we could change the process of natural birth. We saw how important it was for the Samaritans to have the Holy Spirit. If having the Holy Spirit was important for the Samaritans, it was also important for the Ethiopian. I believe he received the Holy Spirit. Irenaeus, an early church father who lived between AD 130-202, wrote that the rejoicing Ethiopian returned to his country and became a missionary to his own people.[34]

After Philip baptized the Ethiopian, the Spirit of the Lord caught Philip away, and he was next seen at Azotus, some twenty miles north of the Gaza road (Acts 8:40). Philip continued to preach in all the cities until he came to Caesarea. We can be certain that everywhere Philip went he preached the same gospel that he preached in Samaria. The same was said of Peter and John on their way back to Jerusalem from the revival in Samaria. They preached in many Samaritan villages (Acts 8:25). We can be certain that they preached the apostles' doctrine. If it was important for the

repentance to Life

Samaritans to be baptized in Jesus' name and filled with the Holy Spirit, we can be certain it was just as important for the people in these other towns and villages. The examples that are recorded are authority enough for us to be obedient to the Scriptures.

The apostles preached Jesus and the people believed: they repented, they were baptized in Jesus' name, and they drank of the Living Water, which is the Holy Spirit evidenced by speaking with tongues. "Let him who hears say, 'Come!' And let him who thirsts come. Whoever desires, let him take the water of life freely" (Revelation 22:17).

chapter twelve

Paul's Conversion

Paul's Conversion

in this chapter, we will consider several passages of Scripture that are important in understanding Paul's conversion. The first passage is Acts 9:1-19. Breathing out murderous threats against followers of the Way, Saul obtained letters from the Jewish council authorizing him to seize these people and bring them to Jerusalem for trial.

Earlier in this study we examined the characteristics of a disciple of the Lord. A disciple was a person who followed Jesus Christ and obeyed His commandments as taught by the apostles. Acts 2:42 said, "They continued steadfastly in the apostles' doctrine"; they adhered closely to it.

Paul was determined to persecute the disciples of Jesus, both men and women. Later Paul characterized his motivation for hunting his quarry as "zeal" and "rage": "I was zealous toward God as you [the Jews] all are today. I persecuted this Way to the death, binding and delivering into prisons both men and women" (Acts 22:3-4). In his testimony to Herod Agrippa II, Paul said, "Many of the saints I shut up in prison . . . and when they were put to death, I cast my vote against them. And I punished them often in every synagogue and compelled them to blaspheme; and being exceedingly enraged against them, I persecuted them even to foreign cities" (Acts 26:10-11).

As a Pharisee, Paul was nurtured in the Scriptures. He did not however, believe that Jesus was the Messiah, the Savior of the world.

repentance to Life

He passionately believed in God and he persecuted the follower of Jesus in the name of God, but he did not believe that Jesus was God in the flesh. Jesus had told other Pharisees (whose beliefs were like Paul's), "If you do not believe that I am He, you will die in your sins" (John 8:24). There is only one "I AM," and Jesus professed to be Him. If Paul were ever to be saved, he would have to come to this understanding of Jesus or he would die in his sins.

Breathing out murderous threats against the disciples of Jesus, Paul journeyed to Damascus. Suddenly, an intense light blinded him, and he fell to the ground, dropping his bundle of arrest warrants. Disoriented, he heard a majestic voice thundering from the heavens: "Saul, Saul, why are you persecuting Me?" (Acts 9:4). Trembling with fear and awe, Saul asked, "Who are You, Lord?" The Lord answered, "I am Jesus, whom you are persecuting."

Paul had received his Pharisaical education under Gamaliel, an eminent doctor of the law. He believed in the "I AM," in Yahweh, the one true Lord. He recognized the voice thundering from the heavens as Yahweh, so he was bewildered when the Lord asked, "Why are you persecuting Me?" Paul had thought that by destroying the heretical rabble he was defending the One whom he loved so fiercely. He was suddenly afraid of the answer to his question, "Who are You, Lord?" The Lord answered, "I am Jesus." As the Sanhedrin's brightest and boldest, Paul immediately realized that his zeal had been misdirected and that he should now embrace Jesus as Lord. The Scriptures he thought he knew intimately would have to be relearned. His allegiance to the Sanhedrin must now be transferred to the followers of the Way. Blind, weak, and in shock, Paul asked, "Lord, what do You want me to do?" (Acts 9:6). The Lord told him to go into Damascus and He would send someone to tell Saul what to do.

Those traveling with Saul stood like statues when the man fell to the ground in terror. They heard thunderings from the heavens and knew Saul was in crisis. Afterward, they helped him up and—realizing that the light had blinded him—led him to the house of Judas on Straight Street. After three days, a disciple named Ananias came to visit Saul. He said, "Brother Saul, the Lord Jesus, who appeared to you on the road as you came, has sent me that you may receive your sight and be filled with the Holy Spirit" (Acts 9:17). Ananias laid his hands on Saul and prayed for him. Scales fell from Saul's eyes, and his sight was restored. Ananias baptized Saul. Saul spent many days in fellowship with the very disciples he had wanted to annihilate. When Saul repented, both Jesus and the disciples forgave him. After all of Jesus' arguments with and teaching to the hardheaded, self-righteous Pharisees, one was finally converted!

Saul believed in Jesus when the light struck him down, but Saul was not converted until he was born again. You can believe in Jesus, but if you do not have the Holy Spirit, Christ does not dwell in you or you in Him (Romans 8:9). If you do not partake of His flesh and blood, you have no life in you (John 6:53). If you are not born of the water and the Spirit you cannot enter the kingdom of God (John 3:5). When it came to salvation, Paul was no different from any other person since the Day of Pentecost. Ananias told Saul he needed to be baptized and receive the Holy Spirit, and Saul obeyed.

Later, in his testimony to the Jews, Paul revealed more of what Ananias had said to him: "The God of our fathers has chosen you that you should know His will, and see the Just One, and hear the voice of His mouth. For you will be His witness to all men of what you have seen and heard. And now why are you waiting? Arise and be baptized, and wash away your sins, calling on the name of the Lord" (Acts 22:14-16). *The Amplified New Testament* reads, "Rise and be baptized, and by calling upon His name wash away your sins" (Acts 22:16).

repentance to Life

Talmadge French said, "The cry of the heart is for the cleansing that only the worthy name of Jesus provides. Jesus pointed to this when He said: 'Except a man be born of water and of the Spirit, he cannot enter into the kingdom of God.'"[35] French continued, "The power in baptism is, plain and simple, in the saving name of Jesus. . . . We link ourselves in identification with the 'one Lord' by being 'baptized into Jesus Christ,' according to Romans 6:3."[36]

As a disciple who had been taught the commands of the Lord Jesus, Ananias knew what to tell Paul. Jesus had told the apostles that repentance and remission of sins should be preached in His name among all nations (Luke 24:47). Remission of sins is the same thing as washing away your sins and it is done when we are baptized in the name of Jesus. Peter likened baptism to the days of Noah and the waters of the Flood: "And this water symbolizes baptism that now saves you also—not the removal of dirt from the body but the pledge of a good conscience toward God. It saves you by the resurrection of Jesus Christ" (I Peter 3:21, NIV). The pledge of a good conscience comes when we repent and are obedient to Christ's commands.

The Bible does not say at what point Paul received the Holy Spirit. However, we do know that he received it because Acts 13:9 says, "Then Saul, who also is called Paul, filled with the Holy Spirit. . . ." Later Paul wrote to the Corinthians that he spoke with tongues (I Corinthians 14:18). Receiving the Holy Spirit is not optional. The disciples received it on the Day of Pentecost, and after that, everyone who was "added to the church" obeyed the apostles' doctrine of repentance, baptism in Jesus' name, and receiving the Holy Spirit evidenced by speaking with tongues. Yes, Paul believed in Jesus, and Ananias was sent to tell him what to do. Paul needed to be born again and that was done when he was baptized of the water and of the Spirit.

Ananias had told Paul that he was going to be a minister and a witness to Gentiles, kings, and children of Israel of the things he had seen and heard. The most important of those things were the salvation message and the story of his conversion. Now he would minister these things to others.

chapter thirteen

That They May Receive Forgiveness of Sins

paul stood before King Agrippa, giving an account of what Jesus told him on the Damascus road: "I will deliver you from the Jewish people, as well as from the Gentiles, to whom I now send you, to open their eyes, in order to turn them from darkness to light, and from the power of Satan to God, that they may receive forgiveness of sins and an inheritance among those who are sanctified by faith in Me" (Acts 26:17-18).

Paul told King Agrippa how he had been true to Christ's commission: "Therefore, having obtained help from God, to this day I stand, witnessing both to small and great, saying no other things than those which the prophets and Moses said would come—that the Christ would suffer, that He would be the first to rise from the dead, and would proclaim light to the Jewish people and to the Gentiles" (Acts 26:22-23).

Jesus came to those who were living in darkness to shine spiritual light into the lives of all people, whether Jew or Gentile. Jesus told Paul that He was sending him to both Gentiles and Jews, to open their eyes in order to turn them from darkness to light, from the power of Satan to God, that they could receive forgiveness of sins and an inheritance among those who are sanctified by faith in Him.

Up to this point, the groups that had received forgiveness and an inheritance of sanctification in Jesus were the Jews and the Samaritans but not the Gentiles. (The Ethiopian Philip had

repentance to Life

baptized on the road to Gaza was the exception.) The Jews who were followers of the Way were of the opinion that this gospel was meant for them alone and that anyone who wanted to be saved had to convert first to Judaism. Even though they looked down on the Samaritans, the Samaritans were part Jewish and their religious practices were similar to Jewish ones. But the Gentiles were in an entirely different category. The Jews considered the Gentiles as "dogs" on account of their many impurities and abominations.[37] (See Matthew 15:26; Acts 10:14.)

Therefore, even though many Old Testament proclamations had declared that God's salvation was for all people, including the Gentiles (e.g., Genesis 12:3; I Chronicles 16:23-24; Psalm 145:8-12; Isaiah 62:2), the Jews who had received the gospel ignored these declarations. Until Peter and Paul received the revelation that God was no respecter of persons, prejudice and tradition kept the Jews from perceiving God's will.

Paul wrote, "For you are all sons of God through faith in Christ Jesus. For as many of you as were baptized into Christ have put on Christ. There is neither Jew nor Greek, there is neither slave nor free, there is neither male nor female; for you are all one in Christ Jesus. And if you are Christ's, then you are Abraham's seed, and heirs according to the promise" (Galatians 3:26-29).

What is an inheritance? How does one receive an inheritance? There is more than one meaning of the word *inheritance*, but the one I feel that is appropriate here is "birthright." *Birthright* means "any right or privilege to which a person is entitled by birth."[38] The Jews were of a natural birth from the seed of Abraham and were a nation chosen by God. God called Abraham out from his country and from his family, to go to a Promised Land that God would show him. God would make from him a great nation (Genesis 12:1-3). The Promised Land was a land flowing with milk and honey, a land that to this day the Jews still claim as theirs.

They are the seed of Abraham, and we Gentiles have no right by inheritance to this land.

However, there is a greater inheritance than the Promised Land. Abraham looked for a better country, a city whose builder and maker was God (Hebrews 11:10). This was a country every nation under heaven could claim through Jesus Christ. This great kingdom of God was not an earthly country corrupted by sin or a nation that constantly divided its love and worship between Yahweh, their King and deliverer, and the gods of other nations. No, God wanted a holy city populated by holy people called by His name; He did not care what nationality they were as long as they loved Him enough to take on His name and to keep His commandments. This inheritance could come only through Jesus Christ, and that was done by a spiritual birth. All people, whether Jew, Samaritan, or Gentile, could gain citizenship to this country through being born again.

Jesus promised that if we would eat His flesh and drink His blood we would live forever. Jesus gave His flesh and blood as an offering for our sins; by this one offering He "perfected forever those who are being sanctified" (Hebrews 10:14). It is through the blood of Jesus that we have remission of those sins (John 6:51-56; Matthew 26:26-28).

To partake of an inheritance, one must be born (or adopted) into the family to which the inheritance is given. And the testator has to die. Jesus Christ, the testator, or the One who wrote the covenantal contract, offered Himself as a sacrifice in order that we might live. He taught and commissioned the apostles to tell all the nations how they could partake in this inheritance. We have seen that the apostles obeyed Christ's commands by teaching disciples about the new birth: repentance, baptism in Jesus' name, and receiving the Holy Spirit. Paul also likened this spiritual birth to the Spirit of adoption (Romans 8:15).

repentance to Life

Paul wrote, "How shall we who died to sin live any longer in it? Or do you not know that as many of us as were baptized into Christ Jesus were baptized into His death? Therefore we were buried with Him through baptism into death, that just as Christ was raised from the dead by the glory of the Father, even so we also should walk in newness of life. For if we have been united together in the likeness of His death, certainly we also shall be in the likeness of His resurrection" (Romans 6:2-5).

Just like Christ was buried after He died, we were buried with Him in baptism after we repented, or died to our old life of sin. Our old nature was "buried," and we were free from sin's taskmaster. That is why Peter associated baptism with the remission of sins and why Ananias told Paul to be baptized to wash away his sins. We are baptized in Jesus' name because we take on His likeness in our burial. We are partaking of His flesh and blood. His blood covers our sins. When we are reborn, we take on our Father's name, the name that is above all names. We must also take on the likeness of His resurrection, and that is done through receiving His Spirit. Jesus gives the baptism of the Holy Spirit because it is necessary for us to be "resurrected" so we can walk in the newness of life.

Paul wrote, "But you are not in the flesh but in the Spirit, if indeed the Spirit of God dwells in you. Now if anyone does not have the Spirit of Christ, he is not His. And if Christ is in you, the body is dead because of sin, but the Spirit is life because of righteousness. But if the Spirit of Him who raised Jesus from the dead dwells in you, He who raised Christ from the dead will also give life to your mortal bodies through His Spirit who dwells in you" (Romans 8:9-11).

When we partook of His death in baptism, we died to sin. When we received His Spirit, we were resurrected into newness of life. Jesus would have stayed in the grave if the Spirit had not resurrected His body. That same principle applies to us. We can be baptized into death, but until the Spirit comes into our "dead" body, we do not have life.

So, to receive forgiveness of sins and an inheritance among those who are sanctified by faith in Jesus, we must be born again. Paul said it did not matter if we are Jew or Greek; we are one in Christ Jesus. By faith, we are Abraham's seed and heirs according to the promise. "For as many as are led by the Spirit of God, these are sons of God. For you did not receive the spirit of bondage again to fear, but you received the Spirit of adoption by whom we cry out, 'Abba, Father.' The Spirit Himself bears witness with our spirit that we are children of God, and if children, then heirs—heirs of God and joint heirs with Christ, if indeed we suffer with Him, that we may also be glorified together" (Romans 8:14-17).

chapter fourteen

You Are Abraham's Seed, and Heirs

"and it shall come to pass that whoever calls on the name of the LORD shall be saved. For in mount Zion and in Jerusalem there shall be deliverance, as the LORD has said, among the remnant whom the LORD calls" (Joel 2:32). Paul quoted this verse: "Whoever calls on [invokes] the name of the Lord shall be saved" (Romans 10:13). So far the Jews and the Samaritans were the only groups to partake of this promise of spiritual birth. There was one more major group that was not yet called by His name: the Gentiles.

Jesus said that He was the way, the truth, the life, and the door and that no one could come to the Father but by Him. There was no exception to the rule or a lesser gospel for the Gentiles; they too had to repent, be baptized in Jesus' name, and be filled with the Holy Spirit.

I love the account of the Gentiles becoming heirs according to the promise along with Abraham's seed. This excites me because it gives me hope. We were not His people, but the Lord said, "You are my people!" and in my soul I am proclaiming, "You are my God!"

Isaiah wrote, "I revealed myself to those who did not ask for me; I was found by those who did not seek me. To a nation that did not call on my name, I said, 'Here am I, here am I'" (Isaiah 65:1, NIV). This prophecy was fulfilled in Acts 10 when the Gentiles received the promise. This group took on the name of God in salvation. "Salvation is found in no one else, for there is no

repentance to Life

other name under heaven given to men by which we must be saved" (Acts 4:12, NIV).

Acts 10 marked an important turning point in the Book of Acts. Up to this time, those who were scattered by persecution from Jerusalem had been preaching the gospel mainly to Jews (Acts 11:19). At this point, the gospel message was opened to the Gentiles.

Cornelius was a Gentile of Italian descent. He and his family were God-fearers, similar to the Ethiopian man Philip had encountered on the road to Gaza. He gave generously to anyone in need, prayed always, and was well respected by the Jewish community in Caesarea. Caesarea was situated about thirty miles north of Joppa on the Mediterranean coast. Cornelius was a centurion in the Roman army, commanding one hundred men.

One afternoon as Cornelius was praying, an angel appeared to him and said, "Your prayers and your alms have come up for a memorial before God. Now send men to Joppa, and send for Simon whose surname is Peter. He is lodging with Simon, a tanner, whose house is by the sea. He will tell you what you must do" (Acts 10:4-6). Note that the angel did not tell Cornelius how to be saved; the apostles—not angels—had been commissioned to do so. Note also that even though Cornelius was a devout, generous man, he and his household still needed to be born again in order to be saved. (Despite Cornelius's goodness and generosity, he was still "unclean." See Acts 10:14.)

Cornelius's household was not yet saved. As noted in the last chapter, they were not Abraham's seed, but they were still heirs according to the promise. This nation was not yet a nation called by His name, but that would change.

At about the same time Cornelius's messengers journeyed toward Joppa, Peter went to the rooftop of Simon the tanner's house to pray. (Maybe it was the only place in the house that caught the fresh sea breeze to waft away the unpleasant smell of his host's trade!) Peter did not yet know it, but God was about to prepare him to open the door of salvation to the Gentiles.

Peter's stomach growled as he prayed; he could not wait to eat. Unexpectedly, he fell into a trance and saw a strange sight that looked like a sheet tied at its four corners. The large bundle seemed to be full of living things because lumps and bumps fluttered and squirmed about. When the bundle landed on the rooftop, Peter saw that it contained all kinds of four-footed animals, reptiles, and birds. Then he heard a voice: "Rise, Peter; kill and eat" (Acts 10:13). According to Moses' law, Jews could not eat unclean animals, and though he was hungry, Peter's stomach rebelled at the thought of chewing and swallowing the meat of an unclean animal, reptile, or bird. (Maybe one of the animals he saw in the sheet was an unclean mongrel!) "Not so, Lord! For I have never eaten anything common or unclean," Peter replied, puzzled at why God would order him to disobey the dietary law. "What God has cleansed you must not call common," said the voice. This same order-and-refusal was repeated three times until the unsavory bundle disappeared into the heavens. While Peter still pondered the strange vision, the Spirit told him that three men had arrived and that Peter was to go with them because God had sent them.

With the vision fresh in his mind, Peter went to the door and greeted the men. "We have come from Cornelius the centurion. He is a righteous and God-fearing man, who is respected by all the Jewish people. A holy angel told him to have you come to his house so that he could hear what you have to say" (Acts 10:22, NIV).

This incident sounds a lot like the story of Paul's conversion. In a vision, Paul had seen a man named Ananias coming and laying hands on him to receive his sight, and he would also tell him what he must do. At the same time, God had prepared Ananias for his mission to Saul, the persecutor. Both Ananias and Peter were commanded by God to go. They would not have gone on their own

repentance to Life

if the Lord had not shown them it was His will. Since Paul was a persecutor of the disciples and Cornelius was an unclean Gentile "dog," normally the Jewish disciples would have avoided both Saul and Cornelius. The Lord knew in both incidents that Ananias and Peter were going to need convincing to do the tasks they were commissioned to do. Sometimes God asks us to do things we are not sure of, but in the end He always confirms His word.

Peter went with Cornelius's messengers, taking six Jewish brethren with him. While Cornelius waited for them to arrive, he called his relatives and close friends to attend the meeting. He wanted all of his loved ones to hear what Peter had to say. Still uncertain about the advisability of this meeting, Peter said, "You know how unlawful it is for a Jewish man to keep company with or go to one of another nation. But God has shown me that I should not call any man common or unclean. Therefore I came without objection as soon as I was sent for. I ask, then, for what reason have you sent for me?" (Acts 10:28-29). Any other haughty, self-assured Roman centurion might have resented Peter's reference to a Gentile's uncleanness, but Cornelius was too hungry and thirsty for more of God to take offense.

Cornelius told Peter the story of how the angel had appeared to him and given instructions to send for Peter who was lodging at the tanner's house in Joppa. The angel had told Cornelius that when this man came he would speak to Cornelius's household. "Now therefore, we are all present before God, to hear all the things commanded you by God" (Acts 10:33). As Cornelius spoke, everything clicked in Peter's mind: he had the keys to the kingdom, and they should be used to unlock the door to all nations as Jesus had commanded the apostles. He now knew that the vision of the unclean animals in the sheet meant exactly what the voice had said—what God had cleansed was no longer common or unclean.

With renewed purpose and anointing, Peter began to preach.

He told Cornelius and everyone assembled, "In truth I perceive that God shows no partiality. But in every nation whoever fears Him and works righteousness is accepted by Him" (Acts 10:34-35). He told these Gentiles about John the Baptist's mission to announce the Christ to the world and how the apostles traveled with Jesus, hearing Him teach and witnessing His miracles. He told about Jesus' death and resurrection and the forty days during which He taught and commissioned the apostles. Peter said, "To Him all the prophets witness that, through His name, whoever believes in Him will receive remission of sins" (Acts 10:43).

Many Old Testament prophecies promised cleansing from sins. "I will cleanse you from all your filthiness. . . . I will give you a new heart and put a new spirit within you. . . . I will put My Spirit within you and cause you to walk in My statutes" (Ezekiel 36:25-27). "In that day a fountain shall be opened for the house of David and for the inhabitants of Jerusalem, for sin and for uncleanness" (Zechariah 13:1). Jesus commanded the disciples to preach and testify about the only One who could grant remission of sins. Jesus is the fountain that has been opened to us, and through His name, we can receive forgiveness of sins. (See Luke 24:46-49; Acts 2:38.)

Peter had been taught and commissioned by Jesus. Jesus had given him the keys to the kingdom. The Holy Spirit had empowered him to preach; his testimony was true. As Peter preached to Cornelius and his house that day, he could see hope and faith dawning on the Gentile faces. Then the Holy Spirit fell on all who listened, and Peter saw astonishment dawn on the faces of his Jewish friends. For they could hear the Gentiles speaking with other tongues and magnifying God in exactly the same way the Jews had received the Spirit! Peter asked the Jewish brethren, "Can anyone forbid water, that these should not be baptized who have received the Holy Spirit just as we have?" (Acts 10:47). And Peter commanded the Gentiles to be baptized in the name of the Lord. Peter's questions to his Jewish brethren presaged the time when he knew he would have to face the displeasure of the apostolic council and give an account of his actions.

In the face of prejudice and tradition, Peter did not preach a different gospel to the Gentiles than he did to anyone else. And when they heard the gospel, the Gentiles responded in the same way as anyone else who received the Word—with obedience and joy! The gospel was the same for all nations. Everyone who received the Word and repented was commanded to be baptized in Jesus' name, because that is what Jesus had commanded (Matthew 28:19; Acts 2:38).

The importance of Cornelius's baptism rested not only on a series of divine interventions but also on a paradigm shift—the commencement of a new era. Peter had to help the Jewish believers see what had been revealed to him—that all men were heirs to the promise, not just Jews. He told the apostolic council in Jerusalem, "Brothers, you know that some time ago God made a choice among you that the Gentiles might hear from my lips the message of the gospel and believe. God, who knows the heart, showed that he accepted them by giving the Holy Spirit to them, just as he did to us. He made no distinction between us and them, for he purified their hearts by faith" (Acts 15:7-9, NIV). In the next chapter, we will see how the Jews reacted to Peter's revelation.

chapter fifteen

Repentance to Life

Repentance is not optional.

the last chapter explained how the door of salvation was opened to the Gentiles. In this chapter I want to revisit the story using the narrative from Acts 11 because Peter's explanation intrigues me. Peter took the whole salvation story and explained what it meant with words and phrases that applied not only to the Gentiles but to the Jew as well. First, however, I want to begin with a discussion of the reason and inspiration for this book: the phrase "repentance to life" (Acts 11:18).

Repentance means "a reordering of one's thoughts and behaviors in accordance with a claim beyond self . . . a change in direction and location."[39] For example, Peter's sermon on the Day of Pentecost convicted his Jewish listeners, and they asked Peter what they should do about their sin. Peter told them to repent—have a change of mind; think differently about this man Jesus, because He is your Messiah, the Savior of the world.

In New Testament Greek, two words convey the idea of repentance: *metanoéo* and *eoustréo*: "to come back, convert, turn about."[40] "These two words derive their moral content not from Greek, but from Jewish and Christian thought, since nothing analogous to the biblical concept of repentance and conversion was known to the Greeks. *Metanoéo* presents repentance in its negative aspect as a change of mind or turning from sin, while *epistrépho*

repentance to Life

presents it in its positive aspect as turning to God. Christ's call to repentance . . . is addressed, not as in the OT to the nation, but to the individual."[41]

Unfortunately, for many repentance means merely feeling sorry when they have done something wrong and been apprehended, or expressing sorrow for causing harm to someone else. "While sorrow may accompany repentance, sorrow does not have the ability to transform life. . . . Repentance is turning from one lifestyle and turning toward another one. Biblical repentance required turning from a life directed by self or others to a life oriented toward God."[42] To feel sorry for one's sins is only part of the repenting process. "Now the person needs to reorient toward the One who can both empower the change and provide a moral example for the new life."[43] Anyone can have good intentions or even try to form new patterns of behavior, but this alone does not provide the power one needs to change his or her direction for all of life. That is why repentance includes a "recognition of divine authority; it is the surrender to the lordship of Jesus Christ."[44] Repentance is essential for salvation. It is the first step on a new life journey that will lead to everlasting life.

Jesus is the One who deliverers from sin and its insidious effects and excuses; He is the One who pardons us and sets us free. Jesus is the One who looses us from the bondage and limitations of sin and empowers us to walk in newness of life. He is the One who opens up for us a whole new world of behavior and hope that both allows and requires change. Before He ascended, Jesus commissioned the apostles to preach to all nations repentance and remission of sins in His name.

In Acts 2, Peter was the first apostle to put Jesus' words into action. He told the convicted Jews to "Repent, and let every one of you be baptized in the name of Jesus Christ for the remission of sins; and you shall receive the gift of the Holy Spirit"

Repentance to Life

(Acts 2:38). Peter preached the same essential message to Cornelius's house. It was by Peter's preaching the gospel and through the faith of the house of Cornelius that God granted unto them repentance to life. The Holy Spirit fell upon all those who heard the word. The Jews who had accompanied Peter heard the Gentiles speak with tongues and magnify God in the same manner they had received the Holy Spirit. Peter commanded the Gentiles to be baptized in the name of Jesus Christ.

The Spirit fell on those who heard the word because they believed Peter's gospel message. The same results can and do occur today. However, if you do not believe that people can receive the baptism of the Holy Spirit, then you will not see the same results that the apostles did in the Book of Acts. If in your church the Holy Spirit is not poured out, it is because people do not expect it to happen. Lack of teaching the truth about the Spirit baptism leads to absence of belief in it; the result is that people are not born from above.

We are to be born of both the water and the Spirit (John 3:5). After Cornelius and his house received the Holy Spirit, Peter commanded them to be baptized in Jesus' name. If you have not been baptized this way, then you have not followed the example of the only way everyone in the Bible was baptized. If someone is going to take the authority to baptize others, then it is his responsibility to conform to the divine authority of the biblical examples. It seems to me that someone who has been baptized according to another formula instead of the one found in the Bible should wonder if his baptism remitted his sins.

When the six Jewish men saw Cornelius and his house speaking with tongues and magnifying God, their eyes bugged out and their mouths dropped open. They were amazed that the Holy Spirit was given to "unclean" people. This was the first time they had seen Gentiles receive the Holy Spirit, but it was not the first time they had seen the Holy Spirit being poured out. They immediately recognized what was happening because they heard the Gentiles speaking with tongues. Tongues were the determining factor because speaking with tongues is the initial sign that the Holy Spirit is entering a life.

Peter asked, "Can anyone forbid water, that these should not be baptized who have received the Holy Spirit just as we have?" (Acts 10:47). The Jews acknowledged that the Gentiles had received the same Spirit they had received.

The news of Peter's exhilarating experience in Caesarea had already reached Jerusalem by the time Peter arrived. The Jewish brethren accused him: "You went into the house of uncircumcised men and ate with them" (Acts 11:3, NIV). Not only had Peter gone into a Gentile house, but he had baptized them as well. The hubbub made it appear as though the baptism of a Gentile was considered sacrilegious. The Jews understood fully the implications of baptism; it was not an empty, trivial act or one left up to a convert to decide if he wanted to be baptized.[45] Water baptism was like entering into a legal covenant with the testator and taking on His name. This would make the one who was baptized an heir of the testator.

The apostle with the keys placed the responsibility for the anomaly of Gentile baptism where it belonged: on God. Peter patiently told his Jewish brethren the whole story of his rooftop vision of the sheet loaded with unclean meat and God telling him three times to pick out a few choice morsels to eat. After each of Peter's refusals, the Spirit told him not to call anything God had cleansed common or unclean. He told about Cornelius's messengers and how he had taken six Jewish brethren with him to Caesarea. They all had witnessed the Gentiles receiving the Holy Spirit during Peter's sermon. Peter finished defending his actions with this clincher: "Then I remembered what the Lord had said: 'John baptized with water, but you will be baptized with the Holy Spirit.' So if God gave them the same gift as he gave us, who believed in the Lord Jesus Christ, who was I to think that I could oppose God?" (Acts 11:16-17, NIV). This transferred the argument from Peter's actions to God's.

All at once the Jews' indignant incredulity changed to wonder and awe as they also received Peter's revelation about God's impartiality. They answered, "Then God has also granted to the Gentiles repentance to life" (Acts 11:18).

The expression "repentance to life" probably means "repentance that results in life."[46] Yes, repentance is "unto life." It begins the process of transformation from an unclean, mortal existence to a clean, godly, immortal life. Despair, apathy, anxiety, and shame are replaced by hope, purpose, peace, and love. After a person repents, he begins to learn how to follow the leading of the Spirit and submit to God's will and Word. He finds strength by joining with a community of believers who live with similar purposes. He focuses his thoughts, attitudes, and relationships *away* from the old life and *toward* the new life.[47] No wonder Paul called this transformed life "a new creation" in Christ (II Corinthians 5:17).

This opportunity for a transformed life had now come to the Jews, the Samaritans, and the Gentiles. As Paul told the Greeks in Athens, "God . . . now commands all men everywhere to repent" (Acts 17:30). (See II Peter 3:9.) Truly, repentance leads to life.

chapter sixteen

The Gentiles Should Hear the Word

Baptism in Jesus' name is not optional.

the gospel that was preached to the Jews and the Samaritans was the same for the Gentiles. It had the same benefits and blessings. Paul wrote, "For this reason I, Paul, the prisoner of Christ Jesus for you Gentiles—if indeed you have heard of the dispensation of the grace of God which was given to me for you, how that by revelation He made known to me the mystery . . . which . . . has now been revealed by the Spirit to His holy apostles and prophets: that the Gentiles should be fellow heirs, of the same body, and partakers of His promise in Christ through the gospel" (Ephesians 3:1-6).

Even though Peter and Paul offered extensive explanations about the "mystery" of God accepting the Gentiles as heirs along with the Jews, certain Jews still thought that Christianity should remain as a sect within Judaism. In other words, these Judaizers thought that Christians should have to convert to Judaism at the same time they were converted by believing and obeying the gospel. The Judaizers did not understand the grace of God. Even today it still takes time to understand God's grace. Since he wrote so much about this subject, Paul's writings are a good place to go to understand what God did for us through Jesus Christ.

Paul wrote to the Galatians who were under pressure from the Judaizers to be circumcised. Paul told the Galatians that rejecting the gospel of grace would cause them to revert back to dependence on Mosaic law and would put them back into bondage. It would change the entire orientation of salvation away from God's grace to their own actions. If the Galatians submitted to circumcision, then they would be obligated to obey the whole law. They would become estranged from Christ. However, if they continued in the grace of the gospel, they would enjoy intimacy with Christ and be justified by faith in Him. They could walk in the way of the Spirit and be heirs of Christ.

Paul explained that in the age of grace, circumcision of the flesh meant nothing any more. Instead of outward circumcision, both the Jews and Gentiles needed their hearts circumcised. God accepted both the Jew and the Gentile in a different way now: through obedience to the gospel; that is, repentance, baptism in Jesus' name, and receiving the Holy Spirit. Paul explained it this way to the Colossians: "For it pleased the Father that in Him [Jesus] all the fullness should dwell, and by Him to reconcile all things to Himself, by Him, whether things on earth or things in heaven, having made peace through the blood of His cross. And you, who once were alienated and enemies in your mind by wicked works, yet now He has reconciled in the body of His flesh through death, to present you holy, and blameless, and above reproach in His sight—if indeed you continue in the faith, grounded and steadfast, and are not moved away from the hope of the gospel which you heard, which was preached to every creature under heaven, of which I, Paul, became a minister" (Colossians 1:19-23).

The Jews were in the same soup as the Greeks—no one could keep the whole law; none were righteous and all had sinned (Romans 3:9-18). If a man broke one law, it was the same as if he had broken them all. The law condemned us as sinners but could never give us remission for our sins. Jesus took away that burden of guilt by His death, burial, and resurrection. We are reconciled to God by obeying the gospel and being born from above. Peter told the apostolic council, "So God, who knows the heart, acknowledged them by giving them the Holy Spirit, just as He did to us, and made no distinction between us and them, purifying their hearts by faith. . . . But we believe that through the grace of the Lord Jesus Christ we shall be saved in the same manner as they" (Acts 15:8-9, 11).

In Acts 16, the Philippian authorities threw Paul and Silas in jail for casting a demonic spirit out of a slave girl. Her masters had charged the two preachers with troubling the city and depriving them of their rightful profit since their slave could no longer tell fortunes. The magistrates ordered that Paul and Silas be beaten with rods and commanded the jailer to keep them securely. The jailer followed orders by putting the two battered preachers in the inner prison with their feet in stocks. Then he went to bed.

At midnight, the derelicts, murderers, thieves, and thugs could not sleep because of the ruckus; their two new dungeon mates were singing. Suddenly the noise turned to rumbles, creaks, groans, and rattles, as the ground shook, their chains fell off, and the prison doors burst open. Jolted from sleep, the jailer ran to the dungeon door and gasped in terror when he saw it gaping open, hanging by one hinge. Knowing what would happen to him if the prisoners had escaped, he drew his sword to kill himself. Paul yelled, "Do yourself no harm, for we are all here." Trembling with shock, the jailer called for a light, ran in, and fell down before Paul and Silas. He asked, "Sirs, what must I do to be saved?" (Acts 16:30).

Paul and Silas replied, "Believe on the Lord Jesus Christ, and you will be saved, you and your household" (Acts 16:31). The jailer knew nothing about Jesus Christ. He only knew that Paul and Silas were not like the other prisoners; the charge against them had been for preaching. When the jailer saw what God did

repentance to Life

in that prison, he knew he needed Him. Paul and Silas's reply was no different from Peter's to the Jews on Pentecost, from Philip's to the Samaritans, or from Peter's to Cornelius; they all had to first believe on the Lord Jesus Christ to be saved.

The jailer took Paul and Silas to his home, where he tended to their wounds. Paul and Silas preached Jesus Christ to the jailer and his family, and the jailer and his house were baptized. Rejoicing, they all sat down to eat together (another example of Jews hobnobbing with Gentiles!).

The gospel Paul preached was the same as the one Peter preached. We can take the statement that the jailer "believed in God with all his household" (Acts 16:34) to mean the same as Peter's statement about the Gentiles: "God gave them the same gift as He gave us when we believed on the Lord Jesus Christ" (Acts 11:17).

In the last chapter we saw that repentance was not optional, and now we see that water baptism in Jesus' name is just as essential to salvation. The purpose of water baptism in Jesus' name is to remit—wash away—sins (Mark 1:4; Acts 2:38; 22:16). By being baptized in Jesus' name, the believer participates in the death and burial of Jesus Christ, a similitude of His death (Romans 6:4; Colossians 2:12). We are baptized "into Christ" by being baptized in His name (Galatians 3:27). The Pharisees' rejection of baptism was characterized as rejecting the counsel of God (Luke 7:30). Water baptism is essential; it saves us. (See Mark 16:16; John 3:5; I Peter 3:21.)

When we believe in Jesus Christ, our journey of faith does not stop there. We will obey the gospel by repenting, being baptized in Jesus' name, and receiving the Holy Spirit. Then we will rejoice!

chapter seventeen

Did You Receive the Holy Spirit When You Believed?

*Baptism in Jesus' name and
receiving the Holy Spirit
are not optional.*

in this chapter,

I would like to focus on Paul and the gospel he preached. In previous chapters we looked at other preachers—Peter, Philip, Ananias—and how the Lord used them to preach the saving gospel message. I find Paul's message to be no different than the others.

In Peter's sermon on the Day of Pentecost, he taught repentance, baptism in Jesus' name for the remission of sins, and receiving the Holy Spirit (Acts 2:38). Another time he said, "Repent therefore and be converted, that your sins may be blotted out, so that times of refreshing may come from the presence of the Lord" (Acts 3:19). In this verse Peter said the same thing as he had in chapter 2, but worded differently. He spoke of repentance, and the blotting out of our sins is done in baptism in the name of Jesus. The "refreshing" meant the Holy Spirit. Peter preached the same gospel message to Cornelius and his house. The Gentiles received the Holy Spirit and they were baptized in Jesus' name.

Philip preached the same gospel to the Samaritans: they were baptized in Jesus' name, and they received the Holy Spirit, and when Peter and John laid hands on them, they received the

repentance to Life

Holy Spirit. After Paul's encounter with Jesus on the Damascus road, Ananias came to preach to Paul and laid hands on him to receive the Holy Spirit. Ananias commanded Paul to be baptized to wash away his sins, and he did it in the name of Jesus.

So we come to Paul. After Paul was converted, he immediately started preaching. I want to start with the disciples of John that Paul found in Ephesus, even though he did not go to this city on the western coast of Asia Minor until his second and third missionary journeys. This handful of disciples (about twelve men) had already repented and been baptized according to John the Baptist's teaching. Paul could tell by their appearance and behavior that they had an experience with God. So he asked, "Did you receive the Holy Spirit when you believed?" (Acts 19:2). They replied, "We have not so much as heard whether there is a Holy Spirit." Paul asked, "Into what then were you baptized?" They answered, "Into John's baptism."

Because Paul wanted to know how these believers had been baptized, we know that not only is baptism essential but also it must be administered according to the gospel as Jesus commanded the apostles. Then Paul explained, "John indeed baptized with a baptism of repentance, saying to the people that they should believe on Him who would come after him, that is, on Christ Jesus" (Acts 19:4). If baptism in Jesus' name were not essential, Paul would not have taken pains to find out how these believers were baptized and then explain the gospel of Jesus Christ to them. When these disciples heard the gospel, "they were baptized in the name of the Lord Jesus" (Acts 19:5). Paul opened the eyes of these men to a greater understanding than they had. Yes, they had been obedient to John's preaching and baptism, but One had come who was greater than John: Jesus Christ.

Paul preached baptism in Jesus' name, just like Peter, Philip, and Ananias. All of the other apostles did as well. Paul did not preach his own gospel but was obedient to the commandments of Christ. If these Ephesian men had to be re-baptized in Jesus' name, so did everyone else who was baptized by John. And if this applied to these men, then it applies to everyone else.

These men had to be re-baptized because remission of sins is obtained only through Jesus Christ. Baptism in Jesus' name has the same meaning as John's baptism of repentance: the remission of sins. But John's baptism was simply to prepare believers to receive Jesus Christ, the Savior. In order for sins to be remitted, the pure, sacrificial blood of Jesus Christ had to be shed. The Ephesians had to be re-baptized—this time in Jesus' name—in order to partake of the flesh and blood of Jesus.

Paul was not yet finished, because he asked the Ephesians if they had received the Holy Spirit. They had not even heard about it. Paul opened their understanding about that also because it was essential to their salvation to be born of the Spirit. "And when Paul had laid hands on them, the Holy Spirit came upon them, and they spoke with tongues and prophesied" (Acts 19:6). If anyone asked them now, they could say they had been born of the water and the Spirit, and they were partakers of the inheritance with those who were sanctified by faith in Jesus Christ.

When these twelve men heard the gospel, they believed, were baptized in Jesus' name, and received the Holy Spirit. This spiritual birth made them the seed of Abraham, and they were justified by faith in Christ Jesus. Later Paul wrote a letter to the church that had been established in Ephesus and described what Jesus had done for them when they obeyed the gospel. "Blessed be the God and Father of our Lord Jesus Christ, who has blessed us with every spiritual blessing in the heavenly places in Christ. . . . In Him we have redemption through His blood, the forgiveness of sins, according to the riches of His grace. . . . In Him also we have obtained an inheritance, being predestined according to the purpose of Him who works all things according to the counsel of His will. . . . In Him you also trusted, after you heard the word of truth, the gospel of your salvation; in whom also, having believed, you were sealed with the Holy Spirit of promise" (Ephesians 1:3, 7, 11, 13).

Paul wrote these passages of Scripture to the twelve original men and the others who had been added to the church. They all trusted in the word that was spoken to them, and because they trusted, they believed in the One John had said would come, the One about whom Paul preached: Jesus Christ. When the Ephesians were baptized, they received redemption through His blood, which was remission of sins, and when they received the Holy Spirit, they were sealed with the Holy Spirit of promise.

We also are admonished to be baptized with the Holy Spirit, the same promised Holy Spirit that the people in the Book of Acts received. It was not just for them but for all who are afar off, as many as the Lord will call (Acts 2:39). "The Lord is not slack concerning His promise, as some count slackness, but is longsuffering toward us, not willing that any should perish but that all should come to repentance" (II Peter 3:9). We can trust in this promise or any promise in the Word of God. Our concern and desire should be that we want to receive this promise.

Paul's gospel was consistent with the apostles' gospel. He required the Ephesians and everyone else who heard him preach to repent and be baptized in Jesus' name. The very fact that Paul laid hands on these men to receive the Holy Spirit tells us that it is important to have.

If God gave the Ephesians the Holy Spirit evidenced by speaking with tongues, why would He not give this good gift to all men in the same manner? Jesus said, "If you then, being evil, know how to give good gifts to your children, how much more will your heavenly Father give the Holy Spirit to those who ask Him!" (Luke 11:13). The Ephesians did not ask to speak in tongues; they were hungry for the promised Holy Spirit. When they received it, they spoke with tongues.

Everyone who received the Holy Spirit in the Book of Acts spoke with tongues. No one ever received it any other way. If God had given the Holy Spirit in various ways, hard feelings, boasting, confusion, or worse would have been the result. Now, if people are receiving the Holy Spirit a "different way" than the way God poured it out, it is because they have not been taught that they can receive the promise in the same manner they received it in the Bible. This principle also applies to baptism. If people are being baptized any other way than in Jesus' name, deceitful unbelievers have misled them. Further, I contend that if someone has received the Holy Spirit in a "different way" than the biblical way or has been baptized "another way" than the biblical way, they do not actually have the Holy Spirit dwelling in them, and their sins have not been washed away.

Even in the early church, false teachers attempted to dissuade some from believing and obeying the gospel. Around AD 48, Paul wrote to the Galatians, "I marvel that you are turning away so soon from Him who called you in the grace of Christ, to a different gospel, which is not another; but there are some who trouble you and want to pervert the gospel of Christ. But even if we, or an angel from heaven, preach any other gospel to you than what we have preached to you, let him be accursed. As we have said before, so now I say again, if anyone preaches any other gospel to you than what you have received, let him be accursed" (Galatians 1:6-9). "The Galatians had unwittingly fallen for a different message, one which was not another true message of salvation at all. Those causing the trouble were guilty of seeking to pervert the gospel of Christ, not to present a better alternative."[48]

repentance to Life

Ultimately, we are all accountable before God for ourselves. If we have the ability to read, we can see the gospel truth in the Scriptures for ourselves, or God can send one of His followers to help us if we really want to know and do what is right.

The Ephesian men received the one and only gospel, and it was no different from the gospel Paul preached to anyone else. I did not have to wonder how God was going to give the Holy Spirit to me, with tongues or without. I knew that when I asked Him for the Holy Spirit, He would give it to me just like He did on the Day of Pentecost when it was first poured out.

Now I want to turn our attention to other examples of Paul's preaching. "And he departed from there [the Jewish synagogue in Corinth] and entered the house of a certain man named Justus, one who worshiped God, whose house was next door to the synagogue. Then Crispus, the ruler of the synagogue, believed on the Lord with all his household. And many of the Corinthians, hearing, believed and were baptized" (Acts 18:7-8).

As was his custom, when Paul first entered a city he would attend the synagogue and preach the gospel of Jesus Christ to the Jews. As in other cities, he persuaded some of the Corinthian Jews and Gentile God-fearers, but some of the Jews so violently opposed Paul that he turned his attention to the Gentiles. We find in this passage of Scripture the words "believed on the Lord," "believed," and "were baptized." The question is: was Paul's message to the Corinthians any different than what he had taught the Ephesians? Let us examine the two examples.

First, we will look at baptism. Paul re-baptized the Ephesians because John's baptism was a baptism of repentance in preparation for the coming of the Messiah. Paul reminded these disciples that John had told them they should believe on the One who would come after him, that is, on Christ Jesus. When they heard this, they were baptized in the name of the Lord

Jesus. When the Corinthian believers were baptized, do you think Paul himself, or Silas and Timothy who were with him, administered baptism any other way than how the Ephesians were baptized?

Paul laid hands on the Ephesians, and they received the Holy Spirit, speaking with tongues. Do you think Paul preached the same message to the Corinthians that he preached to the Ephesians? Yes, the Corinthians had to believe on the One who came after John, who was Christ Jesus. They had to be baptized in Jesus' name, and they had to receive the Holy Spirit from the One who gave it. When Paul laid hands on repentant believers who desired to receive the Holy Spirit, the sign that God had come to abide in them was that the Spirit enabled them to speak with tongues.

The Spirit-inspired men who wrote the Bible did not have to spell out every example of spiritual birth in detail for us to understand what happened. So when we read that certain ones "believed on the Lord" and "were baptized," we understand by other verses of Scripture about baptism that the believers were baptized in Jesus' name. We also understand what happened when we read that certain ones "believed on the Lord" and received the Holy Spirit by referencing other verses of Scripture on that subject. John said that believers would receive the Holy Spirit when they believed on the One who would come after him, the Holy Spirit baptizer, Jesus Christ. (See John 1:33.)

Apollos was another example concerning salvation. He was an Alexandrian Jew, a disciple of John, and a knowledgeable, persuasive speaker. After Paul had established a church in Corinth, he sailed across the Aegean Sea, taking two of his helpers, Aquila and Priscilla, with him. They docked in Ephesus, and Paul could not resist visiting the synagogue to reason with the Jews before he continued his journey toward Jerusalem. He left Aquila and Priscilla in Ephesus, and they were attending the synagogue when the visiting Apollos was invited to speak to the assembly. Touched by Apollos's eloquence and ability to connect with the crowd but also wanting to give Apollos an opportunity to believe on the One who came after John, "they took him aside and explained to him the way of God more accurately" (Acts 18:26).

Remember that when Paul later returned to Ephesus he explained the way of God more accurately to the disciples of John he found there, re-baptized them in Jesus' name, and they were filled with the Holy Spirit. Aquila and Priscilla were part of Paul's evangelistic team. When they took Apollos aside, it would be reasonable to assume that just like Paul did for the Ephesians, Aquila and Priscilla would also teach Apollos the gospel of Jesus Christ, re-baptize him in Jesus' name, and the Lord would fill him with the Holy Spirit. What applied to one applied to all.

In Thessalonica, Paul and Silas gravitated toward the synagogue and preached Christ to the Jews and God-fearing Gentiles. "And some of them were persuaded; and a great multitude of the devout Greeks, and not a few of the leading women, joined Paul and Silas" (Acts 17:4).

In Berea, they again reasoned with the Jews and God-fearers in the synagogue. The Bereans were "more fair-minded" than the Thessalonicans, because they more readily received the gospel and searched the Scriptures daily to corroborate Paul and Silas's message. "Therefore many of them believed, and also not a few of the Greeks, prominent women as well as men" (Acts 17:12).

In Athens, Paul spoke to the Epicurean and Stoic philosophers on the Areopagus, the hill dedicated to Mars, the god of war. This was where the Athenians held court concerning questions of religion and morals. Paul at first captivated his audience's attention because, pointing to a certain altar, he told them he knew the identity of the "unknown god" of that altar. He began to describe Him as the Creator and life giver. However, when Paul broached the subject of the resurrection of the dead, the Greeks turned away from this "babbler." Yet "some men joined him and believed, among them Dionysius the Areopagite, a woman named Damaris, and others with them" (Acts 17:34).

If, as he wrote the Acts of the Apostles, Luke had included every detail of every event, the Bible would be huge, overstuffed with repetition. Just because Luke did not write out every detail does not mean that we cannot deduce what happened in the above events. Consider baptism. Paul and his fellow ministers baptized in Acts 18 and 19. Since this detail is missing from chapter 17, does it mean that he did not baptize the believers in Thessalonica, Berea, and Athens? No, I think they believed and were persuaded to obey the gospel of repentance, baptism in Jesus' name, and receiving the Holy Spirit, just as the Ephesians and Corinthians obeyed. If people want to know how Paul baptized, they turn to Acts 19. If they want to know if Peter baptized the same way as Paul, they go to Acts 2 and 10.

In Acts 2, 10, and 19 are three salvation events in which baptism in Jesus' name and receiving the Holy Spirit as evidenced by speaking with tongues are all the same and described in detail. Three detailed accounts are enough evidence to establish the truth of the apostles' doctrine. In the Old Testament, a man could be convicted of a sin or put death only if two or three witnesses corroborated the charges. (See Deuteronomy 17:6; 19:15.) In the New Testament, Paul applied this principle to witnesses of the gospel message: "By the mouth of two or three witnesses every word shall be established" (II Corinthians 13:1).

A fourth "witness" is in Acts 8, the Samaritan revival. Luke provided the detail that the Samaritans were baptized in the name of the Lord (Acts 8:12, 16). But he omitted that the Samaritans spoke with tongues when they received the Holy Spirit. Great joy had filled the city as a result of their repentance, baptism in Jesus' name, and the miracles wrought through Philip. But no one had received the Holy Spirit. How did they know? Because both Philip and the Samaritans he had taught were looking for the evidence, the sign that the Holy Spirit had entered their lives. This sign was speaking with tongues. When Peter and John arrived and laid hands on the Samaritans, they received the Holy Spirit. How did they know the moment they received the Holy Spirit? They saw and heard something so phenomenal that even Simon the sorcerer was so impressed he offered to buy the ability to perform this "trick." This phenomenon had to be speaking with tongues. Therefore, I offer Acts 8 as the fourth witness of the veracity of the apostles' doctrine.

We are all saved by the grace of God through our faith in Jesus Christ. When we hear the true gospel preached, we are baptized in Jesus' name and receive the Holy Spirit, evidenced by speaking with tongues. The people in all of the examples in Acts 17 were born again because they believed and obeyed an apostle (sent one) who preached the apostles' doctrine, which is the gospel of Jesus Christ.

chapter eighteen

Conclusion

Conclusion

the best gift God gave humankind was Jesus Christ, who purchased our redemption. He also gave every man a measure of faith (Romans 12:3) and a measure of grace (Ephesians 4:7). Other gifts listed in Ephesians 4 were apostles, prophets, evangelists, pastors, and teachers (Ephesians 4:11). Much of *Repentance to Life* has been about these gifts, because many of the above-mentioned men were inspired by the Holy Spirit to write the Bible. They wrote of the Old Testament characters and events that pointed to and culminated in the coming of the Messiah, Jesus Christ; they wrote about His birth, life, ministry, death, burial, and resurrection. They wrote about the disciples He taught and trained and the commission He gave to them. They wrote about how the apostles (sent ones) carried out His commission. They wrote letters of instruction, rebuke, and encouragement to the saints who had received and obeyed the gospel message.

Shortly before Jesus ascended, He commissioned the apostles: "All authority in heaven and on earth has been given to me. Therefore go and make disciples of all nations, baptizing them in the name of the Father and of the Son and of the Holy Spirit, and teaching them to obey everything I have commanded you. And surely I am with you always, to the very end of the age" (Matthew 28:18-20, NIV). Mark added, "He who believes and is baptized will be saved; but he who does not believe will be condemned . . . those who believe . . . will speak with new tongues" (Mark 16:16-17).

repentance to Life

Luke added, "Repentance and remission of sins should be preached in His [Christ's] name to all nations . . . I [will] send the Promise of My Father upon you" (Luke 24:47, 49). John said, "Receive the Holy Spirit" (John 20:22). The power and authority behind this commission was Jesus Christ Himself. The fullness of God dwelled in Him; He was God in flesh. He had taught the apostles long and well; they knew what the commission entailed and they knew what the commands were. All they needed was Holy Spirit empowerment to carry out the commission. As promised, that would come on the Day of Pentecost.

The apostles were entrusted with the ministry of reconciliation (II Corinthians 5:18-19). Only through believing, obeying, and adhering to the gospel message the apostles taught can we be reconciled to God. After we have obeyed the gospel, we can celebrate Christ in our lives. We have partaken of His death, burial, and resurrection. The gospel message is for everyone, whether Jew, Samaritan, or Gentile, for all have sinned and need a Savior.

Abraham believed in God and it was counted to him for righteousness. The sign of his covenant with Yahweh was circumcision. Paul explained to the first-century Christians that those who entered into the New Covenant by faith in Jesus Christ were also counted as righteous because God imparted to them His Son's righteousness. Paul likened New Testament baptism to circumcision, a cutting away of the old nature so that Christ's nature could be formed in the believer. When the gospel message was obeyed, Jesus Christ set the believers free from the bondage of the old law and from the bondage of sin. They were free to walk in newness of life.

Paul spent a lot of time teaching concerning the law. The Jewish Christians of that day did not understand that they were saved by grace and not by the works of the law. However, if Abraham had simply believed God and ignored God's command to leave his

Conclusion

kindred to search for a city whose builder and maker was God, his belief would not have counted. Abraham demonstrated his faith by obeying God's commands. Therefore, his obedience to God's commands was what made his faith count for righteousness. In the same way, our faith is counted for righteousness when we obey Christ's commands. Jesus taught His disciples these commands, and just before He ascended, He commissioned the apostles to go into all the world and make disciples. They were to baptize them in His name and teach them to observe all the things He had commanded.

Faith and obedience to God's commands are the keys to our salvation. Faith alone is not enough, and obedience alone is not enough. God ignites faith in our hearts when we hear the gospel of Jesus Christ preached, and this faith kindles a desire to obey what we have heard. Just saying we believe is not enough; we must demonstrate our faith by our obedience.

Peter, the apostle with the keys to the kingdom, preached the keynote sermon on the Day of Pentecost. He (and the other apostles standing with him in agreement) was the first to implement Christ's commission. His sermon was recorded in Acts 2, the culmination of which revealed salvation's plan to the world: "Repent, and let every one of you be baptized in the name of Jesus Christ for the remission of sins; and you shall receive the gift of the Holy Spirit. For the promise is to you and to your children, and to all who are afar off, as many as the Lord our God will call" (Acts 2:38-39).

Hearing and believing the gospel of Jesus Christ bring us face-to-face not only with Him but also with the realization of our sinfulness and need of a Savior. This realization brings tears of godly sorrow. We repent—turn away—from the deeds, habits, and way of thinking of our lower nature and turn toward a relationship with Jesus that, little by little, teaches us to follow the Spirit and empowers us to form new thought processes, godly habits, and productive ways of relating to others in our world. Therefore, after believing, repenting is the first obedient step one must take to demonstrate that faith.

Without faith it is impossible to please God, and He will not reward that faith unless the believer diligently seeks Him (Hebrews 11:6). Just as Abraham, the father of the faithful, demonstrated his faith by diligently seeking for a city whose builder and maker was God, our faith motivates us to take obedient steps in order to please Him. James asked, "What does it profit, my brethren, if someone says he has faith but does not have works? Can faith save him? . . . Thus also faith by itself, if it does not have works, is dead. But someone will say, 'You have faith, and I have works.' Show me your faith without your works, and I will show you my faith by my works" (James 2:14, 17-18). After believing the gospel message and repenting, being baptized in Jesus' name is the next obedient step. Everyone needs to be baptized in the name of Jesus Christ for the remission of sins because He was the Lamb whose pure, sacrificial blood was offered to atone for our sins. The name of Jesus is above every name, and there is no salvation in any other name (Philippians 2:9-10; Acts 4:12). There is no other name by which we must be saved (Acts 4:12).

According to Jesus' commission, the apostles baptized by immersion in the name of Jesus Christ for the remission of sins. We saw examples of this in Acts 2, 8, 10, and 19. Water baptism is what Jesus called being "born of water" (John 3:5), and it is absolutely necessary to gain admittance into the kingdom of God. Baptism in Jesus' name is how one partakes of the death, burial, and resurrection of Jesus Christ. Baptism in Jesus' name is how one enters into the New Covenant with Jesus Christ. (See Matthew 26:26-28; John 6:53-56.) Baptism in Jesus' name is how one's sins are remitted.

Believing, repenting, and being baptized in Jesus' name for the remission of sins are all steps a believer takes by faith. And by

Conclusion

faith he or she receives the promised Holy Spirit. Being born of the Spirit is just as necessary as being baptized in Jesus' name. Being born of the water and the Spirit is the only way to enter the kingdom of God (John 3:5). As we have seen, the evidence of being born of the Spirit is speaking with tongues. (See Mark 16:17; Acts 2:4; 10:46; 19:6.) Speaking with tongues is the "sound" of the wind Jesus spoke of in John 3. He said that everyone who is born of the Spirit makes this sound.

Receiving the Holy Spirit is symbolic of Jesus' resurrection; it is rising to walk in newness of life. As we allow Jesus' nature to develop in our lives, the Spirit produces the fruit of righteousness: love, joy, peace, longsuffering, gentleness, meekness, goodness, faith, and self-control. The Spirit warns, convicts, and corrects us. The Spirit guides, teaches, and encourages us. The Spirit empowers us to become, as the apostles were, ministers of reconciliation. We are now commissioned, as were the apostles, to impart the gospel of Jesus Christ to all the world.

Jesus is still giving the promised Holy Spirit to those who believe and obey the gospel. In the biblical examples, some believed in Christ, were baptized in Jesus' name, and received the Holy Spirit, while others believed, received the Holy Spirit, and then were baptized in Jesus' name. The order of water and Spirit baptism is not important, because Paul said, "There is one body and one Spirit, just as you were called in one hope of your calling; one Lord, one faith, one baptism; one God and Father of all, who is above all, and through all, and in you all" (Ephesians 4:4-6). Being born of water and of the Spirit is all part of one spiritual birth process. However, believing on the Lord Jesus Christ always comes before the baptism of the water and the Spirit.

Records of actual new-birth experiences are found only in the Book of Acts. The Acts of the Apostles includes their preaching and teaching (even the script of some of their sermons), the

repentance to Life

miracles they performed in Jesus' name, and the journeys they took while spreading the gospel. They wrote epistles to saints, people who had already received and obeyed the gospel. The epistles instructed the saints in holy and righteous living, relationships, and subjects such as giving, law and grace, justification, and the second coming of Christ. Therefore, we cannot go to the epistles to find the gospel message, Christ's commissioning of the apostles, how the apostles carried out the commission, or actual sermons and salvation events. We go to the Book of Acts to see how the apostles fulfilled Christ's commission in telling the world how to be saved.

By believing and obeying the gospel, we partake of the inheritance in Christ Jesus. "For you are all sons of God through faith in Christ Jesus. For as many of you as were baptized into Christ have put on Christ. There is neither Jew nor Greek, there is neither slave nor free, there is neither male nor female; for you are all one in Christ Jesus. And if you are Christ's, then you are Abraham's seed, and heirs according to the promise" (Galatians 3:26-29).

If you have been baptized of the water and the Spirit, then you have been baptized into Christ. Then God has granted unto you "repentance to life."

notes

[1] *The Nelson Study Bible, New King James Version*, ed. Earl D. Radmacher (Thomas Nelson Publishers, 1997), 1687.
[2] James Strong, *The Exhaustive Concordance of the Bible* (New York: Abingdon Press, 1965), 832.
[3] *The Nelson Study Bible,* 1983.
[4] Ibid. "The Beloved" was a messianic title referring to Jesus.
[5] Strong, 538, 873.
[6] *Merriam-Webster's Collegiate Dictionary*, 10th Edition (Springfield, MA: Merriam-Webster, Incorporated, 1998), 247.
[7] Ibid., 18.
[8] Strong, 483, 489.
[9] Ibid., 704.
[10] *Merriam-Webster's Collegiate Dictionary*, 56.
[11] Ibid., 593.
[12] Ibid., 162.
[13] Strong, 121.
[14] Ibid., 221.
[15] Rabbi Ben Isaacson and Deborah Wigoder, *The International Jewish Encyclopedia* (Israel: Prentice-Hall, 1973), 277-278.
[16] Strong, 680.
[17] Ibid., 397.
[18] F. Delitzch, *Commentary on the Old Testament in Ten Volumes, Isaiah* (Grand Rapids: William B. Eerdmans, 1986), 300.
[19] Strong, 318, 335.
[20] Ibid., 337.
[21] *The Nelson Study Bible,* 1975.
[22] Strong, 777.
[23] *The Nelson Study Bible,* 1794.
[24] Ibid., 1808.
[25] Ibid.

[26] M. D. Treece, *The Literal Word, Acts* (Shippensburg, PA: Treasure House, 1993), 41.

[27] Ibid., 43.

[28] *The Nelson Study Bible,* 1819.

[29] David M. Howard, Ph.D., *Fascinating Bible Facts: People, Places, Events* (Lincolnwood, IL: Publications International, Ltd., 1992), 157.

[30] *Merriam-Webster's Collegiate Dictionary*, 1150.

[31] Treece, 271.

[32] *The Nelson Study Bible,* 1833.

[33] Ibid.

[34] Ibid., 1834.

[35] Talmadge French, "The Jesus Name Factor," *The Pentecostal Herald*, Special Issue (Hazelwood, MO: United Pentecostal Church, International, 2006), 50-51.

[36] Ibid., 50.

[37] Spiros Zodhiates, Th.D., *The Complete Word Study Dictionary, New Testament* (Chattanooga, TN: AMG International, Inc., 1992, Revised 1993), 899.

[38] *Merriam-Webster's Collegiate Dictionary,* 117.

[39] James A. Littles Jr., "Repentance," *The Pentecostal Herald,* Special Issue (Hazelwood, MO: United Pentecostal Church International, 2006), 54-55.

[40] Zodhiates, 969.

[41] Ibid., 969-970.

[42] Littles, 54.

[43] Ibid.

[44] Ibid.

[45] Treece, 401.

[46] Ibid., 403.

[47] Littles, 54.

[48] *The Nelson Study Bible,* 1969.